EARLY RAILWAY PRINTS

Figure 1

Surely one of the most striking of all images of the railway, this lithograph was the frontispiece of J. C. Bourne's *History and Description of the Great Western Railway* (1846). It shows the locomotive 'Acheron' bursting out of the darkness of a tunnel near Bristol. The excessive height of Great Western tunnel mouths makes this emergence into light somehow more heroic. The stone tracery seems almost to suggest the vault of some vast and ancient cathedral. 'Acheron's' haystack boiler gleams proudly in the light. This locomotive was one of over sixty of the 'Firefly' class, designed by Daniel Gooch and T. R. Crampton, to replace the odd assortment of largely unsuccessful locomotives with which the Great Western began.

Gareth Rees

EARLY RAILWAY PRINTS

A Social History of the Railways from 1825 to 1850

PHAIDON

The book is dedicated to Owen Rees, whose lifelong interest in railways was a delightful feature of the author's upbringing.

Phaidon Press Limited, Littlegate House, St Ebbe's Street, Oxford
First published 1980
© Phaidon Press Limited 1980

British Library Cataloguing in Publication Data

Rees, Gareth
     Early railway prints.
     1. Railroads in art
     2. Prints, English
     3. Prints – 19th century – England
     4. Railroads – England – History – 19th century
     I. Title
769'.4'93850942   NE962.R/

ISBN 0–7148–2039–3

Printed in Great Britain by Hazell, Watson & Viney Ltd., Aylesbury

ACKNOWLEDGEMENTS

The author would like to thank the following for their help and advice in the selection of prints: Lillian Sutton of the National Railway Museum, York; Wendy Sheridan of the Science Museum Library, London; Mr. Woodward of the Great Western Railway Museum, Swindon; Marilyn Soden, Michael Vanns and especially David de Haan of the Elton Collection, Ironbridge Gorge Museum Trust, Ironbridge, Salop. Professor Jack Simmons, George Otley and Mark Ritchie kindly suggested lines of inquiry which the author has done his best to follow. Finally, my thanks go to the staff of Leicester Polytechnic for their suggestions and encouragement.

PRINT SOURCES

All the prints came from the Ironbridge Gorge Museum Trust, Elton Collection, with the following exceptions: Figure 2 and Plates 5, 6, 13, 22, 80, 81, 82, 83 Crown Copyright, National Railway Museum, York. Plates 2, 20, 25, 26, 29, 30, 33, 34, 41, 58, 62 by courtesy of the Science Museum, London. Figure 3 and Plates 46, 53, 54, 72, 73, 74, 75, 77, 78, 79, 85, 91, 92 by courtesy of the Great Western Railway Museum, Swindon.

CONTENTS

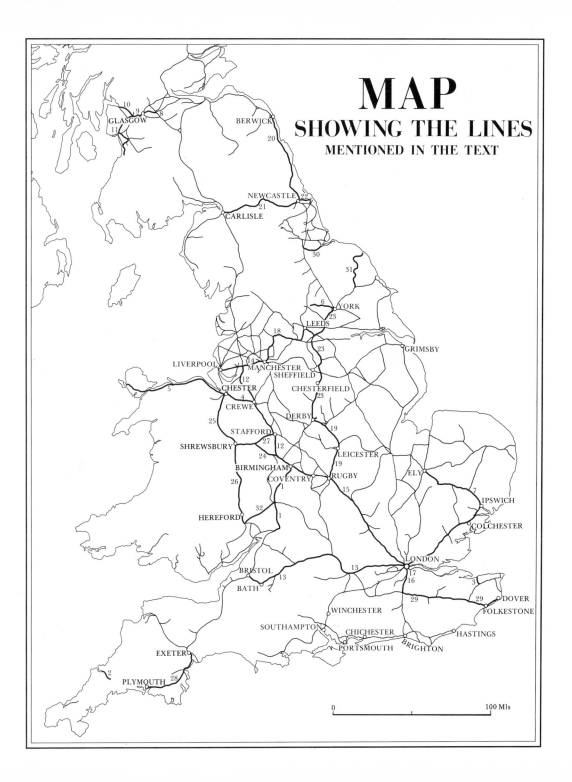

MAP SHOWING THE LINES MENTIONED IN THE TEXT

Figure 2
Stockport Viaduct
London and
   North Western Railway
Artist: A. F. Tait
On Stone by: A. F. Tait
Date: 1848
Tinted Lithograph
Publishers: Bradshaw &
   Blacklock, Manchester

This is the only one of Tait's London and North Western views to be at all well known, through its use as an illustration of mid-nineteenth century industrialization. At the time the view was intended to express admiration of the giant strides of the railway across industrious towns where every inch of space was put to some wealth-producing purpose. To modern eyes, the pollution of water and air are most obvious, while the railway seems to demonstrate the inadequacy of nineteenth-century building controls. Nevertheless, Tait produced in this view something which gave the mid-Victorians a sense of pride and achievement, and in which the railway was paramount.

INTRODUCTION

The building of Britain's railways took place in three phases. The first – with which this book is mainly concerned – lasted from 1830 to the late 1840s and saw the inter-city trunk routes built; the second, from 1850 to the 1870s, involved junctions and cross-country interconnections on the earlier iron skeleton; and the last stage, from the 1880s to 1914, was characterized by long, rural branch lines that penetrated the very heart of the countryside.

The first phase, which coincides almost exactly with the rise of railway prints, was very different in character from the other two. The early companies made large profits on the carriage of valuable freight, reaping a time-saving advantage over canals and roads. As a somewhat unexpected bonus, passenger travel provided as much revenue as freight down to 1850, because the public showed a great desire for travel. The railway was the first means of transport to demonstrate that travel could be enjoyable in itself.

During these first twenty or so years of railway development, the public invested a great deal of emotional as well as financial capital in the iron road. The age was one of great economic and political uncertainty, reflected in violent booms and slumps, unstable prices and employment, and the Chartist unrest that flared up on several occasions. Against this background, the railway was more than a novelty: it was a slowly spreading symbol of change and, it was hoped, progress towards a better world. The railway companies did their best to pay a good return on the confidence placed in them: from the start sound and constant dependability was emphasized in the rigour of timetables, the discipline of rulebooks, the grandiose architectural style of stations and the quasi-military uniforms of the great companies. Even tunnel mouths were embellished to resemble the most impregnable of fortresses.

When Dickens described the upheaval caused by the building of the Camden Town cutting, he perhaps unwittingly reduced to a few words the effects of the first twenty years of the railway age: 'In short the yet unfinished and unopened railroad was in progress, and from the very core of all this dire disorder, it trailed away smoothly upon its mighty course of civilisation and improvement.'

Although only about six thousand miles of track had been completed within the British Isles by the end of the great speculative boom in 1847, the effects of construction on the economy were extensive. Great strains were placed on those industries which supplied raw materials. A mile of double track on the London and Birmingham Railway consumed over two hundred tons of malleable iron in rails alone, and many more tons of cast iron shoes and spikes. A mile of the London and Greenwich Railway's iron rails rested on just over seven thousand granite sleeper blocks of about four cubic feet each. Since the entire line was built on a viaduct, each mile spanned over two hundred arches and required millions of bricks. A mile of the London and Croydon Railway consumed over two thousand pounds worth of timber and over five hundred pounds worth of ballast. Stations and rolling stock placed other heavy demands on the engineering and building industries. If the contemporary economy was unstable, at least railways provided a constant stimulus which largely explains the trebling of iron production and doubling of coal output between the 1820s and the 1840s.

In the mid-1840s railway construction employed about a quarter of a million men, but millions more in supplying industries owed their livelihoods to it indirectly. This engine of growth in the British economy lasted well into the second half of the nineteenth century as railway construction continued in Britain, and also migrated to Europe, India, America and the Dominions. That enthusiastic burst of railway development that swept through Britain between 1830 and 1850 was to be found somewhere in the world right down to 1914.

Once a line was completed, new economic effects became apparent. According to Bradshaw's *Railway Almanack*, just under fifty thousand people were employed as railway servants in 1848. Despite stipulations of literacy and sobriety, the great danger of working on the permanent way, and the fact that hours and wages were no better than in many other occupations, there was great competition for even unskilled railway jobs. The reason for this lay in the security of railway employment. Some companies offered sickness benefits or widows' pensions through mutual societies; others offered company houses at advantageous rents (the Great Western Railway offered both); but all railway companies offered the possibility of promotion up a ladder of graded posts for good employees. Perhaps most important of all, railway employment was immune to the trade cycle. The timetable determined the pace of work, and trains had to run on time whether full or empty. In this sense the railway offered a new and attractive way of earning a living, with job security and a career structure rather than regular bouts of unemployment or short-time working.

With the completion of the main-line network in the 1840s, a national economy was brought into existence for the first time. By reducing travel times to a fraction of what had been possible by road or canal, railways enabled producers to sell goods further afield and draw supplies from hitherto inaccessible regions. Farmers, for example, could buy bulk feeds, fertilizers and heavy machinery, while selling their produce in ever more distant towns. Manufacturers no longer had to keep large stocks of raw materials available in case canals froze or roads became impassable. The railway telegraph, which spread quickly in the late 1830s, put distant buyers and sellers in immediate contact. So the great connecter had the effect of eliminating rural isolation and famine while making the food supplies of the growing cities more secure.

The building of the British rail network involved less state intervention than was to occur in other countries. The role of the state was important at the launching of projected railways, in choosing appropriate routes and in co-ordinating and controlling competition of companies. But the entire system was financed by privately subscribed stocks and bonds, £240 million worth by 1850. The railways did not pioneer such corporate fund raising, the canals had done that, but the scale of operations and the power of the amalgamated companies were larger than that of any other companies in the world at that time. Up to 1846 dividends averaging over six per cent were paid, attracting the savings of the merchant and professional middle classes. While returns were so high, the railways even attracted funds which, in less exceptional times, might have gone into house ownership.

Once built, the railway promoted social responsibility in government. In an age of non-intervention, government found railways too important to leave entirely alone. The need to ensure public safety and convenience led to the establishment of the Railway Department in 1840, and the passing of the Parliamentary Trains Act of 1844, which compelled companies to provide at least one train each weekday at a speed of not less than twelve miles per hour and a fare of not more than a penny a mile. The Department's functions included inspections of tracks, carriages and running speeds; thus railways followed factories and schools in having a full-time inspectorate at a time when laissez-faire dominated government policy.

The social impact of the railway was more immediately obvious than the economic effects outlined above. The sudden increase in speed of communication hit contemporary observers quite forcibly. It was not just that travel times were reduced to about a fifth of fast coaching times (putting all mainland and most Irish stations within a day's travel of London by 1850) — there was also the railway telegraph. Initially intended as a means of communicating advance notice of trains, it was subsequently used as a commercial and social medium as railway companies allowed public access to operators at railway stations. Writing of the seven wonders of the ancient world, Bradshaw's *Railway Almanack* considered that: 'the discovery of the Electric Telegraph has unquestionably added one other to the list.' In a short poem in the same article, the telegraph is addressed as:

> Thou wondrous, whispering wire!
> Thou time and space-annihilating wand!

In the early nineteenth century news travelled so slowly that even month-old copies of *The Times* still had resale value in remote parts of England. Yet by 1842 news travelled so quickly that the government was able to receive intelligence and direct troop movements in response to the Chartist troubles almost on an hourly basis, thanks to the railway telegraph.

The speeds at which people could be moved around or even out of the country are best illustrated by Charles Dickens in his short story *A Flight* (1851). In tones of virtual disbelief, he describes an eleven-hour journey from London to Paris via Folkestone, which ends with a nineteenth-century expression of something between culture shock and jet lag as he wanders the streets of Paris on the evening of the same day he left London Bridge: 'So I pass to my hotel, enchanted; sup, enchanted; go to bed, enchanted; pushing back this morning (if it really were this morning) into the remoteness of time, blessing the South Eastern Company for realizing the Arabian Nights in these prose days.' Trains were capable of speeds around fifty miles per hour by 1850 so it is scarcely surprising that mental adjustment to rapid changes of scene should take a little time.

Fifty miles per hour over rails about twelve feet long (compared with modern sixty-foot rails) must have created an alarming clatter, and Dickens, in the same story gives a vivid and witty impression of breakneck speed:

> Bang! We have let another Station off, and fly away regardless. Everything is flying. The hop gardens turn gracefully towards me presenting regular avenues of hops in rapid flight, then whirl away. So do pools and rushes, haystacks, sheep, clover in full bloom delicious to the sight and smell, corn sheaves, cherry orchards, apple orchards, reapers, gleaners, hedges, gates, fields that taper off into little angular corners, cottages, gardens, now and then a church. Bang, bang! A double-barrelled Station! Now a wood, now a bridge, now a landscape, now a – Bang! a single-barrelled Station – there was a cricket match somewhere with two white tents, then four flying cows, then turnips – now the wires of the electric telegraph are alive, and spin, and blurr their edges, and go up and down, and make the intervals between each other most irregular: contracting and expanding in the strangest manner. Now we slacken. With a screwing, and a grinding, and a smell of water thrown on ashes, now we stop!

Once the possibilities of travel at such speeds were culturally accepted, the railway came to play a part in the redistribution of population from country to town – a process that had started before the industrial revolution. By 1851, about half of the population of England and Wales lived in towns and census evidence seems to indicate an acceleration of this trend between 1831 and 1851. However, it is dangerous to assume that urbanization was promoted by railways in a generalized manner. Some large, country towns which were not dependent on industrial employment, seem to have stagnated or declined in population when the railway arrived – for example, Bath and Cambridge. The arrival of the railway did not only link surrounding countryside to towns, it linked towns to other towns and therefore enabled rapidly growing centres of employment to draw population from less thriving areas. So it appears that the railway only improved the channels of mobility, rather than determined the direction that population movements would take. One safe generalization is that the railway reduced that fear of the unknown which discouraged migration: six million people visited the Great Exhibition of 1851 and London became a known quantity to the many provincial and rural dwellers who took excursion trains to the metropolis for the first time in their lives. Organized travel of any kind broke down prejudices and inhibitions. Moreover, the railway offered the chance of frequent visits home for the worker employed in another town, enjoying opportunities and employment of which he might have remained ignorant without the railway. In these ways the railway helped to calm the fears of those reluctant to be too far from their families and communities of origin.

In one sense the railway imposed a central metropolitan order on the provinces. Before the railways, time had varied throughout the country. As the sun rises and sets rather later in the west than in the east, the day was divided up into hours that ran a little behind those of London in most of the country. However, to make sense of the railway companies' timetables, the railway and telegraph clock became the public regulator. Bristol had been ten minutes behind London, Manchester nine minutes and Glasgow sixteen minutes, but by the late 1840s Greenwich Observatory Clock was being connected with some of the principal railway telegraphs. Despite the fixing of two separate minute hands on some station clocks in the 1840s, one indicating London and one local time, railway (or London) time was becoming standard for all towns by the early 1850s rather than the other way round.

The standardization of time was one obvious result of the railway, but less quantifiable was the tendency to cultural uniformity it promoted. Manners, dress, accent and literature may have been influenced in various degrees, though evidence of a national culture replacing local folkways is hard to uncover. The biography of Thomas Hardy written by his second wife, in which he undoubtedly had a hand, would have us believe that when the railway was extended to Dorset in the mid-nineteenth century, orally transmitted ballads were slain at a stroke by London comic songs. This is clearly an exaggeration, but the railway did promote the circulation of certain types of reading matter and enable London newspapers to reach the provinces on their day of issue. London news could travel even faster. In 1848 a speech by Queen Victoria appeared in a Manchester newspaper only fifteen minutes after telegraph transmission of it was completed. Stock market and financial information travelled in similar manner. The impact of the newspapers should not be exaggerated, however, since paper duty still applied in 1851 and put newspapers beyond the reach of many who could have read them.

The effective monopoly of station bookstalls established by W. H. Smith by the 1850s also promoted a tendency towards a national market in literature. Short novels and magazines, often containing romantic fiction, formed a recognizable genre referred to as 'railway literature'. Railways also carried mail much more quickly than coaches. In fact the influence of the railway on news and literature was such that it is possible to speak of the emergence of public opinion in the mid-nineteenth century and to note the gradual decline of things local, especially dialects and Celtic languages.

In the 1830s and 1840s the railway passed from being an exciting novelty to being so much an accepted part of life as to be unremarkable when it arrived at the few small towns hitherto untouched by it. The opening of the early lines was accompanied by much junketing, most of which was orchestrated by the directors of the railway companies. Commemorative objects were issued to accompany an opening ceremony – medals, tablecloths, jugs, mugs, handkerchiefs and other small souvenirs perhaps aimed at those too poor to travel on trains but who nevertheless had a few pence with which to remember the day.

Several publishers seem to have realized that the opening of a line was worth the issue of a print sold as a single sheet, or, if the market would support it, in a loosely bound book with a few words of introduction. Most views of the Stockton and Darlington Railway (1825) seem to have been made well after the opening, but H. Ward of Canterbury was able to publish a lithograph by T. M. Baynes of the opening of the Canterbury and Whitstable Railway in May 1830 (Plate 1). But the opening of the Liverpool and Manchester Railway in September 1830 proved the commercial possibilities of the railway print. At least four artists made drawings and about thirty different views were ultimately published, ranging in price from a few pence for an individual view to twelve shillings for the first edition of T. T. Bury's *Six Coloured Views on the Liverpool and Manchester Railway*.

From the Liverpool and Manchester Railway onwards, scarcely a line of note was opened in the 1830s without some view of its engineering accomplishments being published locally. Railways were receiving the kind of commemorative attention normally reserved for coronations. Indeed, the Great Exhibition of 1851 and the opening of the Liverpool and Manchester Railway, both technological achievements, were treated in much the same way as state ceremonies by the artists involved. This surely indicates the attitude of the early Victorians to technology: a confidence and belief in progress not held since that time. In the later thirties and forties, more lavish volumes of railway prints appeared, resembling the topographical works popular since the eighteenth century, and containing introductions drawing attention to antiquities adjacent to or visible from the line. The railway itself, which had occupied the foreground of the Liverpool and Manchester Railway prints, was actually absent from some views as artists concentrated on what could be seen from the line. In other views the railway was a distant part of a scene in which older topographical conventions of landscape had reasserted themselves. After the collapse of the railway mania in 1847 – the first shaking of confidence in the financial integrity of the railway – views of bridges and other engineering feats associated with railways became important.

In all, perhaps two thousand different railway prints were published in the twenty years from 1830. This figure requires some explanation. Nothing much is known of the numbers of copies published of each print, but the large collections at York, Ironbridge and London, and nineteenth-century bibliographies, publishers' catalogues and booksellers' lists seem to indicate that there are something of the order of two thousand different views. There are great problems in defining what constitutes a railway print. Many townscapes include a viaduct or a distant plume of steam that has made them of interest to the railway-print collector, though they say little of the railway itself. Pocket railway guides, often issued at very low prices in series under publishers' names like Drake, Roscoe, Freeling or Measom, often contained minute vignettes and woodcut engravings of railway scenes; the *Illustrated London News* did the same on a larger scale after 1850. Railway and engineering periodicals occasionally produced small copper-plate engravings by way of technical explanation or even as a free gift to subscribers. All these have been disregarded and the estimate of two thousand refers to prints published as objects in themselves rather than as embellishments to a text.

Most of the prints were lithographs. The railway was indeed fortunate in having at its service a new technology of illustration whose flourishing roughly coincided with the first two decades of railway development. The most famous railway print publisher of the 1830s, Rudolf Ackermann, was a pioneer of lithography in England. A minority of prints were aquatints, and an even smaller number were produced by other intaglio processes such as etching and copper line engraving.

The relationships between the various people involved in the production of railway prints are complex but important to an understanding of the extremes of quality the prints reveal. The names to be found underneath prints can be misleading. An artist would make a drawing on the spot 'from nature' which was then transferred to a stone for a lithograph or to copper or steel for an engraving. J. C. Bourne and A. F. Tait performed these processes themselves, but T. T. Bury and J. W. Carmichael, both of whom used intaglio processes, left it to others to do their engraving and clearly owe a great deal to such people. S. G. Hughes, T. Picken and L. Haghe, all of whom appear frequently as sculptors or engravers to better-known artists, worked for firms of lithographers or for themselves. Among the best known of these firms of lithographic printers were Ackermann, Day and Haghe, and Hullmandel. To make matters still more complicated, these lithographic printers occasionally acted as publishers, as did booksellers. For example, William Spreat of Exeter, who was involved in Dawson's views of the South Devon Railway, had a lithographic press, a small publishing business and a bookshop. To sum up, there were four distinct functions in print production: original artwork, transfer to the printing medium, lithographic or intaglio printing, and publishing. It is tempting to suppose that the best quality prints emerged where those involved covered more than one stage: Bourne drew 'from nature and on stone', and Ackermann printed and published. Louis Haghe appears to have performed all four functions at different times.

Over two hundred prints appeared in book form, accompanied by an introduction to or commentary on the line illustrated in the plates. The best known of these volumes are, in chronological order:

Thomas Talbot Bury, *Six Coloured Views on the Liverpool and Manchester Railway*, 1831

I. Shaw, *Views of the Most Interesting Scenery on the Line of the Liverpool and Manchester Railway*, 1831

A. B. Clayton, *Views on the Liverpool and Manchester Railway*, 1831

Henry Booth, *An Account of the Liverpool and Manchester Railway*, 1831

David Octavius Hill, *Views of the Opening of the Glasgow and Garnkirk Railway*, 1832

R. Clayton, *Thirteen Views on the Dublin and Kingstown Railway*, 1834

Andrew Nichol, *Five Views on the Dublin and Kingstown Railway*, 1834

G. F. Bragg, *Six Views on the London and Greenwich Railway*, 1836

J. E. Jones, *Six Views on the Dublin and Drogheda Railway*, 1836

H. Belcher and G. Dodgson, *Illustrations of the Scenery on the Line of the Whitby and Pickering Railway*, 1836

James Wilson Carmichael, *Views on the Newcastle and Carlisle Railway*, 1836

Thomas Talbot Bury, *The London and Birmingham Railroad*, 1837

John Cooke Bourne, *Drawings of the London and Birmingham Railway*, 1839

W. E. Trotter, *The Croydon Railway with its Adjacent Scenery*, 1839

W. W. Young and Louis Haghe, *Illustrations of the Great Western and Bristol and Exeter Railways*, 1840

Arthur Fitzwilliam Tait, *Views on the Manchester and Leeds Railway*, 1845

John Cooke Bourne, *The History and Description of the Great Western Railway*, 1846

Other prints appeared as sets but were probably not published in book form: for example, Dawson's views of the South Devon Railway, published in the late 1840s by Spreat of Exeter, and Tait's views on the London and North Western Railway, published by Bradshaw and Blacklock in about 1848. Still more prints appeared as plates illustrating books primarily concerned with engineering feats: for example, George Hawkins's magnificent views of the construction of the Menai railway bridge (see Plates 87, 88, 89 and 90) which appeared with Edwin Clark's *The Britannia and Conway Tubular Bridges*, 1851, or the fine view of Camden Town engine house that was a frontispiece to F. W. Simms's *Public Works of Great Britain*, 1839. Most of the rest were probably issued singly by enterprising publishers in the locality of the scene depicted.

Who actually bought the prints? The publication prices of those prints that appeared in the books named above were high. Only Jones's *Dublin and Drogheda*

Figure 3 (facing page)
The Station at Shrewsbury
(Jointly operated by four Railway Companies)
Artist: Probably I. N. Henshaw
On Stone by: J. W. Giles
Date: 1849
Tinted Lithograph
Publisher: Unknown

Shrewsbury was at the centre of a veritable cobweb of railways: the town's name appeared in the titles of twenty-two proposed and realized railway companies during the nineteenth century. A large joint station was built by the Shrewsbury and Birmingham, Shrewsbury and Hereford, Shrewsbury and Chester and the Shropshire Union Railway Companies and was opened by June 1849. The combined resources of the companies produced a handsome station with a platform six hundred feet long, three-quarters of which was covered by a wrought iron roof. The style of the station façade was very reminiscent of an Oxford college with its embattled tower, octagonal turrets and oriel windows. Perhaps the designer of the station, Thomas Penson, intended it to echo the academic traditions of Shrewsbury school.

could have been aimed at a mass market, priced at a shilling for six engravings. Most of the others were over ten shillings (more than a week's wages to an agricultural labourer) and Bourne's *London and Birmingham* was ninety-four shillings and sixpence for thirty lithographs. The fact that so many of the surviving prints have been hand coloured suggests that former owners were wealthy enough to have them coloured for display purposes. They certainly became collectors' items before the end of the nineteenth century; a catalogue of the Birmingham bookseller Edward Baker for 1893 reveals an asking price of over ten pounds for Bury's *Liverpool and Manchester* and forty-two shillings for Henry Booth's *Account of the Liverpool and Manchester*.

The quality of railway prints was highly variable. Many of the artists were quite unfamiliar with what they were drawing, and the earlier prints should not be relied on as sources of technical information, especially when it comes to locomotives. Moreover, any attempt to draw a curving railway line receding from foreground to background required an ability to depict perspective which most of them lacked at that time. Therefore most railway prints are attempts at straight documentary since the subject matter was difficult enough in itself for the artist's eye. Certain artists and lithographers seem to stand out as having greater popularity than others, and to judge from the rate at which their works have been reproduced in books on railways and related subjects, Bourne and Bury are the most attractive.

John Cooke Bourne (1814-96) began making drawings of the construction of the London and Birmingham Railway in 1836 and published his lithographs in four parts jointly with Rudolf Ackermann in late 1838 and early 1839. Later in 1839 the works were published as one volume with a descriptive account by John Britton, who was Bourne's patron. The most interesting feature of the prints was the depiction of a line under construction, not seen in any other contemporary work. Bourne's views of the excavations at Camden Town (see Plate 43) reflect his fascination for the idea of progress, order and civilization emerging from chaos, and the prints are therefore often compared with Dickens's similar reaction in *Dombey and Son*. In the early 1840s Bourne published a few single prints of railway works, usually viaducts, but was commissioned by Charles Cheffins in about 1845 to produce his *History and Description of the Great Western Railway*. Once again there was something unusual in his views, which were published in 1846 – he was depicting a railway that had been open for some years and therefore 'knew what it was doing'. The prints exude confidence, and the landscapes somehow look as though the railway had been part of them for centuries. The tunnels are more like medieval catacombs than new engineering works. The frontispiece shows the book title carved in a cliff above a tunnel mouth, and the letters are overgrown with foliage (Figure 1). Bourne's reputation is certainly justified, though he never returned to railway subjects after the relative failure of his *History of the Great Western Railway*.

Thomas Talbot Bury (1811-77), a pupil of Augustus Pugin, was the artist responsible for the best-known views of the Liverpool and Manchester Railway. Published as hand-coloured aquatints in paper covers by Ackermann in February 1831, Bury's work went through many editions covering a period of about three years. There were seven views in the first edition and thirteen in the second. A reissue appeared in 1832 followed by Spanish and Italian editions, while the prints were reproduced separately in France and Germany. After re-engraving, new editions appeared in England in 1833 and 1834. The many copies and different versions of the Bury prints vary a great deal in the quality of colouring. Ackermann clearly realized the potential of the British and European markets for railway prints as no other work passed through so many editions, yet the engravers S. G. Hughes and H. Pyall probably deserve as much credit as Bury for the finished versions. Bury was clearly in favour of aquatint well into the age of lithography. In 1837 Ackermann published for Bury the first part of what was intended to be a series of views of the London and Birmingham Railway. Variously engraved by Harris, Hunt and Fielding, these six aquatints obviously failed as a commercial venture because no more parts appeared, but they make an interesting contrast with Bourne: Bury's views appear to be drawn from an early and more genteel period of railway development.

Among artists who perhaps deserve more attention are I. Shaw and A. F. Tait. Nothing is known about Shaw, although he was responsible for the artwork of the famous long prints entitled 'Travelling on the Liverpool and Manchester Railway' (see Plates 9 and 10). In 1831 he produced a series of detailed etchings in paper covers. Two sets of four etchings appeared (although three sets were announced), apparently drawn, engraved and published by Shaw. Shaw was a fine and sensitive artist, and in his two locomotive etchings – the 'Planet' (Plate 12) and the 'Northumbrian' (Plate 11) – he gives more detail than in any other contemporary print.

Arthur Fitzwilliam Tait (1819–1905) is well known for his nineteen lithographs of the Manchester and Leeds Railway, published by Bradshaw and Blacklock in 1845. Although finely executed, they say rather more about the countryside around the line than about the railway which, although it appears somewhere in each view, is often so far distant as to be all but invisible. More interesting in many ways is a series of fifteen tinted lithographs at the National Railway Museum, York, which has been largely overlooked in railway illustration. They may have been published by Bradshaw and Blacklock in about 1848 and are collectively titled *Views on the London and North Western Railway*. In content they make the railway integral to the landscape to such an extent that cows graze and labourers go about their business oblivious to huge viaducts that tower above them (see Plate 34). Even canals and turnpikes seem unaffected by the railway.

Among other artists involved in railway prints, Klingender has drawn attention to Dawson and Hawkins, both of whom are associated with particular lines: Dawson with the South Devon Railway and Hawkins with the Chester and Holyhead. Both had spectacular scenery in which to locate their railway views.

How valuable a source of information are railway prints to the study of history? It has already been noted that the first phase of railway construction in Britain coincides with the heyday of the railway print. The examination of railway prints suggests certain emphases to the historian that are not immediately obvious from written sources.

Firstly, railway prints were strong in their advocacy of the railway. Railway construction was opposed by vested interests in canals, turnpikes and landownership, and distrusted because of its dangerous technology. The early accidents, often caused by boiler explosions or breaking rails, collisions, or the collapse of a bridge or cutting, confronted society with the spectacle of sudden and violent death. It was believed initially that to be in a confined space, such as a tunnel, with a locomotive was to risk suffocation. Novelists, in describing railway accidents, emphasized their suddenness and the helplessness of victims in locked carriages. Against this, railway prints stressed the grace and order of the railway in the landscape. Although newly built, railways never looked new in prints and even when Bourne showed a line under construction, the effort seemed somehow heroic. A railway accident, like a prize fight, could attract a print publisher, but in general, artists placed railways in a favourable light. Bury's prints for example, always depict well-to-do people associating with trains in bright sunlight on excessively tidy stations (see Plate 25). Animals near or on trains seem unfrightened by the experience (see Plates 33 and 52). Cuttings and embankments are grassed over (Plate 27), and station crowds well disciplined (see Plates 41, 80 and 94). Although the actual appearance of a railway in its first few years must have been as raw as a new motorway in more recent times, it never appears so (Plates 47 and 51).

Railway prints helped to subdue the alarm felt by ordinary people at the noise, smoke, danger to life, and the very sight of something that apparently moved without natural cause. Railway company directors realized this and encouraged the sale of prints as good publicity for a line. For example, in the preface to Carmichael's *Views on the Newcastle and Carlisle Railway*, it is revealed that the work was 'undertaken at their [the directors'] suggestion'. Since the prints must have been circulated among people who had not yet seen a railway, they must to some extent have prepared the ground for an acceptance of the new technology. For many, the European editions of Bury's *Liverpool and Manchester Railway* may have been the first contact with the very idea of the railway.

Secondly, although there is great danger in accepting the technical detail in railway prints as historical evidence, they do point clearly to the unfinished nature of the evolution of railway technology; and though the triumph of the 'Rocket' at the Rainhill Trials in 1829 is often seen as proving conclusively that locomotives were to be the chosen form of motive power, it was by no means a settled issue. Gradients steeper than one in a hundred in the early 1830s, and perhaps one in seventy in the later part of the decade, were just not possible for contemporary locomotives, which had neither the weight nor the adhesion to pull trains up such inclines. On the Liverpool and Manchester Railway, stationary engines were necessary on gradients that would not today present any difficulties. All the artists involved with the London and Birmingham Railway give great attention to the Camden Town engine house, used to pull trains up the incline from just outside Euston. It is perhaps rather surprising to recall that a major railway company built its London terminus at a point inaccessible to locomotives. The Birmingham and Gloucester Railway was built with a gradient too steep for British locomotives, and special banking locomotives or double-heading arrangements were used on the Lickey Incline right up to the end of the steam age.

Even in the 1840s the locomotive was not so satisfactory as to preclude alternative experiments. The atmospheric system was tried by Brunel, and illustrated by Dawson (Plate 84), on the South Devon Railway in 1847. It was also used on the Dublin and Kingstown Railway from 1844 to 1854 and speeds of sixty miles per hour were claimed. The London and Croydon Railway experimented with it between 1844 and 1847, while the Canterbury and Whitstable Railway used a locomotive, stationary engines and the atmospheric system on different sections at different times. The atmospheric system involved the construction of pumping houses at regular intervals to create a vacuum in a continuous pipe between or alongside the track. The train was attached by an arm to a piston inside the pipe, and an airtight seal was effected by a continuous flap valve. The train was pulled along by the vacuum ahead and atmospheric pressure behind its piston. The system, although much talked about, never worked well because of deterioration of the valve. Since most of the lines on which it was used were single tracks, the problems of passing loops and reversing must have been considerable. Nevertheless, its use indicates that locomotive traction was not necessarily paramount. This point is further illustrated by the way in which some lines, the Whitby and Pickering, and the Stockton and Darlington for example, reverted to horse-drawn trains in preference to locomotives. The Bodmin and Wadebridge Railway, so long cut off from the national network, also reverted to horses. A similar lack of uniformity relates to gauges: the Great Western Railway's seven-foot gauge is well known and appears in many prints (see Plate 79). The Glasgow and Garnkirk Railway was four feet six inches for no obvious reason.

Thirdly, railway prints are a reflection of an unusual stage of British industrialization. When a new technology is in its early stages of development it sometimes strikes the public imagination as something which is going to change the world. This happened in the early days of motor cars, or television, and is happening now with micro-processors. But in the early days of the railway, there was not only a new, high-pressure, steam technology with which to become familiar, there were also great feats of civil engineering to be performed, and most railway prints after the Liverpool and Manchester commemorate the triumph of engineering over obstacles of nature. Huge viaducts, deep cuttings, great bridges and tunnels express the confidence of the age in man's ability to mould the environment to some economic end. Concern for what lay in the path of the railway was minimal in these early days, and the self-confidence of the engineer was absolute. Trevithick's plans for a conical cast iron monument one thousand feet high to celebrate the 1832 Reform Bill is but one example of this. Equally unlikely railways were planned in the mania periods when huge sums of money were lost and gained and there was a rush to submit schemes. Yet railway promoters and engineers climbed the ladder of social respectability with great speed, the middle class became genuinely interested in science as learned societies flourished, while Mechanics' Institutes appeared in many cities at the artisan level. The railway provided an opportunity for the engineer to show what he could do in 'speaking to the condition' of the age. Although railway prints were mass-produced, luxury consumer goods in an age before such things were normally saleable, small wonder that people bought them to link their homes with the better future.

Lastly, railway prints occasionally reflect other aspects of the age. The sharp distinctions made in quality of accommodation for first-, second- and third-class passengers, for example, reflect the emergence of a form of social class distinction with industrialization. Albert Smith, in his novel *Christopher Tadpole* (1848), remarked on the lack of sociability of first-class passengers who, afraid to compromise their dignity by speaking, passed the journey by looking silently out of the window. Second-class passengers, in less luxurious surroundings, were likely to talk in warm weather only, exchanging few pleasantries and 'closing the windows to suffocation' in cold weather. In the third class, the 'rattling open pig pens', rain could be a preoccupation.

> If you turned your back to it, it filled the nape of your neck; if you faced it, you had overflowing pockets, with an additional cataract from the front rim of your hat, which before long was as limp as wet brown paper. Some people covered their heads with handkerchiefs; . . . it was only prolonging the misery as you did not know next where to put your handkerchief when you removed it. Everything was ruined, from your health downwards.

Although most prints show first-class passengers or those invited on opening day, the roof passengers in Carmichael's views of the Newcastle and Carlisle Railway (see Plates 28 and 31) cannot have travelled for purely romantic reasons!

Similarly, variation also occurs in the architectural styles adopted by the different companies. The South Devon Railway chose an Italianate style for its atmospheric engine houses (Plate 49), but the traveller from Devon to London would find no consistency in his journey: at Bristol the train shed roof suggested a Tudor banqueting hall (Plate 54), while neo-classical themes would dominate much of the rest of the journey to London.

Despite the dangers inherent in relying on any work of art as an historical source, railway prints reveal something of the atmosphere and attitudes of the second quarter of the nineteenth century. Although some well-known prints are reproduced in the following pages, the quality of some of the less familiar work deserves consideration. All of them contribute to an understanding of the most revolutionary twenty-year period in British railway history.

SUGGESTIONS FOR FURTHER READING

Barman, C., *Early British Railways*, Harmondsworth, Penguin, 1950

Carter, E. F., *An Historical Geography of the Railways of the British Isles*, London, Cassell, 1959

Coleman, T., *The Railway Navvies*, Harmondsworth, Penguin, 1965

Darby, M., *Early Railway Prints*, London, Victoria and Albert Museum, 1974

Dendy Marshall, C. F., 'The Liverpool and Manchester Railway', *Transactions of the Newcomen Society*, II (1921–2), p. 12

Elton, A., *The Piranesi of the Age of Steam*, Country Life Annual, 1965

Fine Early Railway Prints, London, Phillips Son & Neale, Auction Catalogue, 1977

Hamilton Ellis, C., *Railway Art*, London, Ash & Grant, 1977

Kellett, J. R., *The Impact of the Railways on Victorian Cities*, London, Routledge & Keegan Paul, 1969

Klingender, F. D., *Art and the Industrial Revolution*, Edited and Revised by Sir Arthur Elton, St. Albans, Paladin, 1975

Lewin, H. G., *Early British Railways, 1801–44*, London, The Locomotive Publishing Co., 1925

Lewin, H. G., *The Railway Mania and its Aftermath, 1845–52*, London, The Railway Gazette, 1936

Morgan, B., *Early Trains*, London, Hampton House, 1974

Perkin, H., *The Age of the Railway*, London, Panther, 1970

Reed, M. C., (ed.), *Railways in the Victorian Economy*, Newton Abbot, David & Charles, 1969

Simmons, J., *The Railways of Britain, An Historical Introduction*, London, Routledge & Keegan Paul, 1961

Simmons, J., *The Railway in England and Wales*, Vol. I, *The System and its Working*, Leicester University Press, 1968

LIST OF PLATES

LINE	DATE OF COMPLETION	PRINT
Eastern Counties	1843	View of the River Lea Bridge and Stratford Viaduct *Plate 32* Ely Cathedral *Plate 65*
South Eastern	1844	Tunbridge Wells Station *Plate 64*
London and North Western	1846	Stockport Viaduct *Figure 2* Edge Hill Station *Plate 80* Crewe Station *Plate 81* Crewe Station *Plate 82* Olive Mount *Plate 83*
Shrewsbury and Chester	1848	The Station at Shrewsbury *Figure 3* Chirk Viaduct *Plate 45*
Shrewsbury and Birmingham	1849	The Railway Station at Wellington, Shropshire *Plate 59*
South Devon	1849	View of a Landslip near Dawlish *Plate 46* The Atmospheric Railway at Dawlish *Plate 49* The Viaduct at Ivy Bridge *Plate 50* Dawlish From the Line of the South Devon Railway *Plate 84* Teignmouth in Broad Gauge Days *Plate 85*
East and West Yorkshire Junction	1850	Knaresborough Viaduct *Plate 38*
Chester and Holyhead	1850	Bangor *Plate 61* Britannia Tubular Bridge Over the Menai Straits *Plate 87* Britannia Tubular Bridge, Platform and Construction of Tubes *Plate 88* Britannia Tubular Bridge, the Floating of the Second Tube *Plate 89* Britannia Tubular Bridge Over the Menai Straits *Plate 90*
South Wales	1856	Chepstow Bridge Over the River Wye *Plate 62* Chepstow *Plate 91* Bridgend *Plate 92*
Inverness and Aberdeen Junction	1858	The Viaduct over the River Spey *Plate 95*
Worcester and Hereford	1860	Malvern from the Link Railway Station *Plate 93*
Western Extension of the West Midland (Jointly Operated)	1860	Crumlin Viaduct *Plate 86* The Interior of the General Railway Station, Chester *Plate 94*

THE PLATES

A Note on Sizes
Most of the prints reproduced in this book have been reduced in size. The majority of lithographs were larger than the format of this book in printed surface alone. Perhaps the largest are Hawkins's views of the Menai Tubular Bridge which have printed surfaces of about forty by sixty centimetres. Most aquatints were somewhat smaller than lithographs, having printed surfaces of around twenty by thirty centimetres. Most of the copper and steel engravings were substantially smaller – those reproduced from guides could be as small as eight by twelve centimetres.

View of the Opening of the Stockton and Darlington Railway
Artist: J. Bousefield
Date: 1825
Black and White Lithograph

The first fully public railway, the Stockton and Darlington, grew out of a colliery line. The coal came from pits at Bishop Auckland on a horse-drawn tramway, and the line which joined the two markets for coal, Stockton and Darlington, was the one on which locomotives were used from September 1825. Although the inaugural train pulled up to six hundred passengers, locomotives were restricted to coal trains for many years and passengers were hauled by horses. The Stockton and Darlington was essentially an upgraded colliery line, but steam traction was provided on hundreds of miles of such lines. This lithograph includes what is possibly the earliest view of a passenger train and an inclined plane.

View of the Canterbury and Whitstable Railway from Over the Tunnel, Taken on the Opening Day, May 3 1830
Artist: T. M. Baynes
Lithographer: C. Hullmandel
Date: 1830
Publisher: Ward, Canterbury

Four months before the opening of the Liverpool and Manchester Railway, the Canterbury and Whitstable was opened. It had one locomotive, 'Invicta', and parts of the line were cable-hauled by stationary engine, as in this view. Two celebratory trains took part in the opening and two views were published locally to celebrate the occasion. The line was all that was built of a plan by William James to construct a railway across Kent. It had a single track and never proved very profitable.

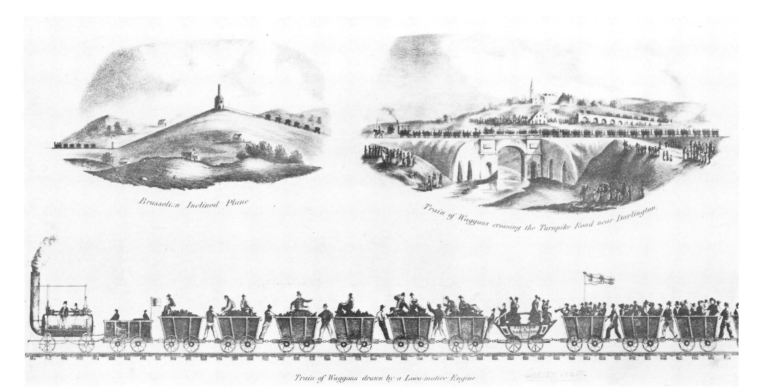

Brusselton Inclined Plane

Train of Waggons crossing the Turnpike Road near Darlington.

Train of Waggons drawn by a Loco-motive Engine.

Views of Trains and Rolling Stock
Liverpool and Manchester Railway
Artist: Unknown
Date: 1830
Black and White Engraving
Publisher: E. Wallis, London

Once the railway existed, inquisitiveness spread in advance of it. London did not have a railway until 1836, but a London publisher produced a rather stylised set of images of rolling stock to satisfy the curiosity. Sir Arthur Elton, from whose collection this engraving is drawn, used the last coach in the top train as his bookplate. The locomotive 'William the Fourth', which is drawing the second train, was one of two built by Braithwaite and Ericsson who had entered the 'Novelty' for the Rainhill Trials. The locomotives were unable to meet the requirements of the directors and were withdrawn by the builders.

The 'Novelty' drawing a Train
Liverpool and Manchester Railway
Artist: C. B. Vignoles
On Stone by: R. Martin
Date: About 1830
Black and White Lithograph

The 'Novelty' was the London-built entrant in the Rainhill Trials of 1829 designed by Braithwaite and Ericsson. It was built in six or seven weeks, financed by Vignoles, and weighed less than three tons. The cylinders were vertical, working upwards, and acted on the rear pair of wheels by means of bell cranks. 'Novelty' was the most successful of the Rainhill failures and was used to some extent in the early days of the Liverpool and Manchester Railway. Charles Blacker Vignoles was involved in an early survey of the line and went on to become a leading railway engineer. When he won a contract in Russia in 1847 he took J. C. Bourne with him as a resident artist.

LIVERPOOL AND MANCHESTER RAILWAY.

Length of Road thirty-one miles.

Average time of Journey one hour and a quarter.

Cost of execution £820,000.

Opened 15th Sept. 1830.

Published by E. Wallis, 42, Skinner-Street, London.

The Moorish Arch from the
  Tunnel
Liverpool and Manchester
  Railway
Artist: T. T. Bury
Engraved by: S. G. Hughes
Date: 1831
From: T. T. Bury, *Coloured Views
  on the Liverpool and Manchester
  Railway*
Coloured Aquatint
Publisher: Ackermann, London

Because the railway was an entirely new departure in technological terms, its projectors seem to
have felt the need to refer to
classical themes in architecture
to provide some cultural point of
reference. The Moorish Arch is
the best example of this on the
Liverpool and Manchester Railway. As Sir Arthur Elton pointed
out in his revision of Klingender's *Art and the Industrial Revolution*, the artist or architect was
concerned to draw a deliberate
parallel with a view of the Gate
of Grand Cairo by Luigi Mayer
in 1802. The Arch was situated
just above the top end of the
tunnel at Edge Hill, Liverpool,
and its real purpose was to house
the two stationary engines used
for drawing trains up from Wapping. There was one engine in
each upright.

Warehouses at the End of the
  Tunnel Towards Wapping
Liverpool and Manchester
  Railway
Artist: T. T. Bury
Engraved by: S. G. Hughes
Date: 1831
From: T. T. Bury, *Coloured Views
  on the Liverpool and Manchester
  Railway*
Coloured Aquatint
Publisher: Ackermann, London

The Liverpool and Manchester
line began close to Queen's
Dock, Liverpool, at Wapping. It
ran in a cutting twenty-two feet
deep and forty-six feet wide to
the entrance of a tunnel which
took the line up to Edge Hill.
The cutting, which contained
four tracks, had various warehouses on cast iron pillars over it
so that goods could be raised and
lowered into waiting wagons,
which in turn could be shunted
about by hand with turntables
and sliding rails. Two men could
move loads over five tons with
the help of these contraptions.
This view shows the tunnel
mouth, the cast iron supports for
the overhead warehouses, and
workmen moving a wagon which
has been turned onto a side line.

The Tunnel (1)
Liverpool and Manchester
   Railway
Artist: T. T. Bury
Engraver: H. Pyall
Date: 1831
From: T. T. Bury, *Coloured Views
   on the Liverpool and Manchester
   Railway*
Coloured Aquatint
Publisher: Ackermann, London

The tunnel from Wapping to
Edge Hill was over two thousand
yards long, twenty-two feet wide
and sixteen feet high. It was built
in seven or eight separate
lengths, with its spoil lifted out
through vertical shafts. Some of
the tunnel roof was natural rock
and some was brickwork, but the
whole roof and walls were
whitened and lit by a gas jet
every thirty yards. This was to
reassure spectators who were
allowed to visit the tunnel and
admire the arches of light and
darkness created by the lighting.
This early print shows a locomotive in the tunnel under steam
which was both illegal under the
conditions of approval of the line
and incorrect since the tunnel
had a gradient of one in forty-
eight and was equipped with
cables to draw trains through it.

The Tunnel (4)
Liverpool and Manchester
   Railway
Artist: T. T. Bury
Engraver: H. Pyall
Date: 1831
From: T. T. Bury, *Coloured Views
   on the Liverpool and Manchester
   Railway*
Coloured Aquatint
Publisher: Ackermann, London

Realizing the potentially embarrassing mistake of showing a locomotive steaming through the tunnel, Ackermann put out a second version in which the chimney of the locomotive had been removed, and then a third in which cables were added. Not until the fourth edition were all signs of the locomotive removed. This amusing affair highlights the extent to which engravings were altered to make them more correct or more up to date. The Liverpool and Manchester prints put out by Ackermann went through so many English and foreign editions that occasionally whole plates were re-engraved.

Travelling on the Liverpool and Manchester Railway
Artist: I. Shaw
Engraver: S. G. Hughes
Date: 1833
Coloured Aquatint
Publisher: Ackermann, London

Perhaps the most famous of all railway prints, this is one of two oblong
plates brought out towards the end of 1831 to complement two already
published sets of six views by T. T. Bury. A slightly altered version
(shown here) appeared in 1833. The upper train is drawn by 'Jupiter',
incorrectly shown with equal-sized wheels, while the lower train is
hauled by 'North Star', an improved 'Rocket', with a primitive
water-barrel tender. In the 1831 edition, the lower train has no
canopies. The upper carriages reflect the style of turnpike coach-
building. The most comfortable passengers would have been those in
the private coach on a flat-bed truck, with benefit of two sets of springs.

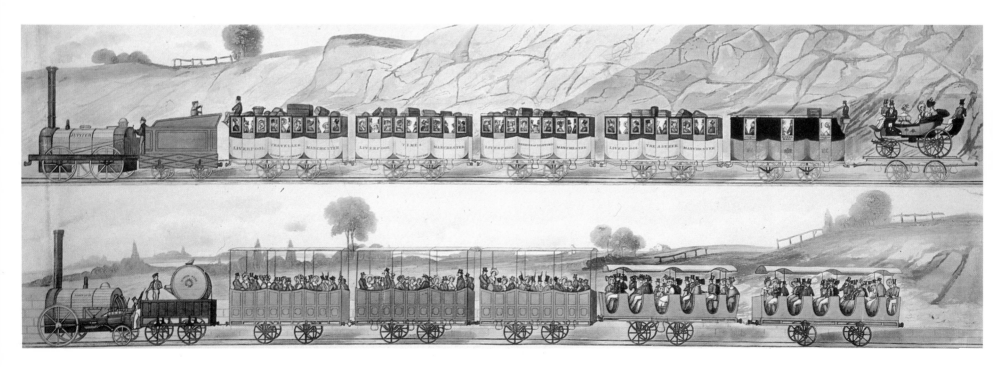

Travelling on the Liverpool and Manchester Railway
Artist: I. Shaw
Engraver: S. G. Hughes
Date: 1894
Chromolithograph
Publisher: Raphael Tuck & Sons, London and New York

Railway prints were already collectors' items by the 1890s when Tuck issued this purported reprint of the 1831 Ackermann aquatint, but the background is quite different. The trains are well copied but the print must be considered a good imitation of the original. The upper locomotive, 'Liverpool', ran on the line for only a short time and never became the property of the company. According to Dendy Marshall, the lower locomotive, 'Fury', is well illustrated. Beneath the print it is made clear that the trains consist of private wagons for which the owners paid tolls as on the roads.

The Northumbrian Engine
Liverpool and Manchester
   Railway
Artist: I. Shaw
Engraver: I. Shaw
Date: 1831
From: I. Shaw, *Views of the Most
Interesting Scenery on the Line of
the Liverpool and Manchester
Railway*
Black and White Etching
Publisher: Shaw, Liverpool, and
   seven others

The 'Northumbrian' was one of eight engines to take part in the opening ceremony of the Liverpool and Manchester; it drew the leading train. It was similar to the 'Rocket' but had less steeply inclined cylinders, and was the first locomotive to have a firebox integral with the boiler barrel, a buffer beam in front and a modern tender (as against a truck with a barrel on it). The engine weighed just over five tons, and consumed about four hundredweight of coal and five hundred gallons of water on a journey from Liverpool to Manchester. Shaw considered it a fourteen horse-power engine and had no doubt that such locomotive engines 'are likely to alter the face of the country, politically, socially and commercially considered.'

The Planet Engine
Liverpool and Manchester
    Railway
Artist: I. Shaw
Engraver: I. Shaw
Date: 1831
From: I. Shaw, *Views of the Most
    Interesting Scenery on the Line of
    the Liverpool and Manchester
    Railway*
Black and White Etching
Publisher: Shaw, Liverpool, and
    seven others

Of all the artists, lithographers
and engravers involved in railway scenes, I. Shaw of Liverpool
was the most ready to draw locomotives in detail. Fortunately, he
chose to include one in each of
his two-part publication of views.
The unsteadiness produced in
fast running by the steeply inclined cylinders of the 'Rocket'
led Stephenson to produce a
second generation of locomotives
in which the cylinders were
almost horizontal. There were
two prototypes: the 'Planet' and
the   'Northumbrian'.   The
'Planet' was the first locomotive
to have its cylinders inside under
the smokebox with the driving
wheels in the rear. It was the
model for about seventeen identical locomotives subsequently
employed on the Liverpool and
Manchester Railway.

Three Views on the Liverpool and Manchester Railway
Artist: S. Kelper
Engraver: J. Harris
Date: 1836
Three Coloured Aquatints
Publishers: Ackermann, London; Lacy, Liverpool

After the Liverpool and Manchester Railway was extended to Lime Street, Liverpool, in 1836, this plate of three views was issued. It shows two views of the new station and one of recently completed work at Edge Hill. It is the last view of the Liverpool and Manchester Railway to be published by Ackermann and is typical of the very high standards of hand-coloured aquatint achieved by his firm.

The Viaduct Across the Sankey
  Valley
Liverpool and Manchester
  Railway
Artist: T. T. Bury
Engraver: H. Pyall
Date: 1831
From: T. T. Bury, *Coloured Views
  on the Liverpool and Manchester
  Railway*
Coloured Aquatint
Publisher: Ackermann, London

About half way between Liverpool and Manchester, the railway crossed the Sankey Valley, through which ran one of the first canals in England. The railway passed over an elegant but simple viaduct of nine arches of fifty feet in span. It was built of brick with stone facings, with about sixty feet of clearance beneath it to allow ample room for the masts of sailing barges on the canal. As the ground beneath the viaduct was soft, about two hundred piles were driven up to thirty feet into the ground beneath each pier. The cost of the viaduct was forty-five thousand pounds.

NEW STATION, LIME STREET.
Entrance to the Tunnel, Booking-Offices &c.

EDGE HILL STATION.
End of the Tunnel.

NEW GRAND ENTRANCE TO THE LIVERPOOL AND MANCHESTER RAILWAY, LIME STREET, LIVERPOOL.

Rainhill Bridge
Liverpool and Manchester Railway
Artist: I. Shaw
Engraver: I. Shaw
Date: 1832
From: I. Shaw, *Views of the Most Interesting Scenery on the Line of the
     Liverpool and Manchester Railway*
Black and White Etching
Publisher: Shaw, Liverpool, and seven others

Rainhill Bridge was a popular subject in the early railway age for two
reasons. Firstly because it was on the level portion of line to either side
of it that the Rainhill Trials were held in October 1829. On this
occasion the possibility that locomotives could offer great advantages
over fixed engines was first demonstrated. Secondly, the bridge had
some constructional distinctions of its own. It carried the Liverpool and
Warrington Turnpike over the railway at an acute angle. The total cost
of the erection of this skew bridge was nearly four thousand pounds,
and of the sixty-three bridges on the line it was perhaps the most
elegant.

Chat Moss
Liverpool and Manchester Railway
Artist: I. Shaw
Engraver: I. Shaw
Date: 1831
From: I. Shaw, *Views of the Most Interesting Scenery on the Line of the
     Liverpool and Manchester Railway*
Black and White Etching
Publisher: Shaw, Liverpool, and seven others

The crossing of Chat Moss involved the building of a 'floating'
embankment nearly five miles long, across a boggy fen. This was the
greatest engineering difficulty faced in the construction of the line, and
took three years to complete. It was originally proposed to dig the
bottom out of the fen and fill it up with soil until a solid roadway was
possible, but the ultimate solution was a floating bed. In the words of
Shaw, 'the railway, for the most part, floats on the surface of this
healthy ocean; and where it was softest, branches, brushwood, and
hurdles formed by twigs and heath, twisted and plaited in frames, were
made a foundation, floating by their buoyancy, which was afterwards
covered with two or three feet of sand and gravel. When these had
become sufficiently compact, on them were placed the wood sleepers
and rails . . .' Shaw's enthusiasm for this accomplishment was almost
boundless: 'Scarcely are there any difficulties, however great, which
cannot be surmounted by genius, industry, and perseverance.'

The Opening of the Bodmin and Wadebridge Railway
Artist: C. Ingrey
On Stone by: C. Ingrey
Date: 1834
Hand-Coloured Lithograph

Opened on 30 September 1834, the complete twenty-mile line with two locomotives and forty wagons cost only thirty-five thousand pounds. Because the line was not linked to the rest of the rail network until late in the nineteenth century, it remained very much in its original state. A charming pair of its early carriages can be seen at the National Railway Museum, York. This view shows the 'Camel' engine pulling twenty-two carriages containing more than four hundred people over Pendevy Bridge.

The Tunnel, from the excavation, looking towards Dublin
Dublin and Kingstown Railway
Artist: Andrew Nichol
Engraver: John Harris
Date: October 1834
From: A. Nichol, *Five Views of the Dublin and Kingstown Railway*
Aquatint in black and blue, hand colouring added
Publishers: Wakeman, Dublin; Ackermann, London; Tilt, London;
   Hodgson, Boys & Graves, London

The Dublin and Kingstown Railway received authorization in 1831 for its six miles and was the first railway in Ireland. On a short extension to Dalkey, the atmospheric system was used from 1844 to 1854, the first experiment with it in the British Isles and the only one to last more than a few months. Before 1841 the railway used locomotives built by G. Forrester of Liverpool; both examples in this view appear to be travelling in the same direction.

Olive Mount
Liverpool and Manchester Railway
Artist: I. Shaw
Engraver: I. Shaw
Date: 1832
From: I. Shaw, *Views of the Most Interesting Scenery on the Line of the Liverpool and Manchester Railway*
Black and White Etching
Publisher: Shaw, Liverpool, and seven others

In order to disarm opposition to the railway, its approaches to Liverpool were kept as unobtrusive as possible. A mile and a half from Liverpool station was Olive Mount Cutting, a deep, narrow ravine seventy feet deep and nearly two miles long. The spoils removed from Olive Mount were used to build an embankment to carry the line across the Roby Valley.

View of the Liverpool and Manchester Railway at the Point where it crosses the Duke of Bridgewater's Canal
Artist: A. B. Clayton
On Stone by: F. Nicholson
Printed by: J. F. Cannel, Liverpool
Date: 1831
From: A. B. Clayton, *Views on the Liverpool and Manchester Railway*
Black and White Lithograph
Publisher: Engelmann, Craf, Coindet et Cie

This view of some rather fanciful third-class coaches behind a barrel-tender locomotive is more interesting historically than technically. It was one of three views by Clayton, a lesser known artist of the line. It shows the line crossing the Bridgewater Canal, the first spectacularly successful investment of the eighteenth-century canal age. Just as the canal halved the price of coal in Manchester overnight, so the Liverpool and Manchester Railway halved the passenger fare. For the whole journey the price dropped from ten shillings by road to five shillings by rail. The journey time fell from four or five hours to sixty to ninety minutes. Not surprisingly, the work of four or five hundred horses and their attendants was no longer required. The two most renowned undertakings of the canal and railway ages met at this point.

View from the Surrey Canal
London and Greenwich Railway
Artist: G. F. Bragg
On Stone by: G. F. Bragg
Date: 1836
From: G. F. Bragg, *Six Views of the London and Greenwich Railway*
Coloured Lithograph
Publisher: Ackermann, London

This was London's first railway. It received approval in 1833, reached Deptford in 1836 and Greenwich in 1838. It also demonstrated a number of important lessons: firstly, it was only just under four miles long yet it saved up to fifty minutes over turnpike traffic using a parallel route; secondly, it showed how many people a railway could move in and out of a crowded city. In its first year of operation it carried nearly one and a half million passengers, not including season-ticket holders, and as many as twenty-five thousand in one day.

View from the Back of the
   Greenwich Road
London and Greenwich Railway
Artist: G. F. Bragg
On Stone by: G. F. Bragg
Date: 1836
From: G. F. Bragg, *Six views of the London and Greenwich Railway*
Coloured Lithograph
Publisher: Ackermann, London

Although double tracked, the railway was built entirely on a single viaduct from close to London Bridge. Many houses were demolished to make way for it. This became a common occurrence in London where the railway provided an excuse for slum clearance. Later the viaduct grew wider as the line was shared with other rail companies seeking access to London, and today it carries twelve sets of rails. The viaduct arches were intended for use as houses but were found suitable for storage only. Initially the line was carried on stone sleepers.

View near Proven Mill Bridge looking West, Opening of the Glasgow
  and Garnkirk Railway
Artist: D. O. Hill
On Stone by: D. O. Hill
Lithographers: W. Day, London
Date: 1832
From: D. O. Hill, *Views of the Opening of the Glasgow and Garnkirk Railway*
Black and White Lithograph
Publisher: Hill, Edinburgh.
Sold by: Tilt & Ackermann, London

This view shows what Hill describes as the 'artificial valley' through
which the railway passed, east of Proven Mill Village, near Glasgow. It
also shows the temporary accommodation for the navvies who built the
line – a row of thatched dwellings on the embankment to the right. The
locomotive is again 'St. Rollox', this time conveying the directors and
their friends on the morning of the opening. Before numerous spectators, another train of thirty-two carriages is travelling westwards
behind the locomotive 'George Stephenson'. Despite the enthusiasm of
the passengers, the line was one of the few on which freight revenues,
principally coal, vastly outweighed passenger revenue in subsequent
years.

View of the Depot looking South
Glasgow and Garnkirk Railway
Artist: D. O. Hill
On Stone by: D. O. Hill
Lithographers: W. Day, London
Date: 1832
From: D. O. Hill, *Views of the Opening of the Glasgow and Garnkirk Railway*
Black and White Lithograph
Publisher: Hill, Edinburgh
Sold by: Tilt & Ackermann, London

David Octavius Hill, later a
pioneer photographer, was encouraged by a friend to make
drawings of the opening of this
line on 27 September 1831, and
later to publish them 'for the
gratification of the directors and
shareholders'. Work began on
the eight-mile line in 1827, and
the final cost was nine thousand
pounds a mile. The rails were
carried by cast iron shoes on
stone blocks, each weighing three
hundredweight. Timber sleepers
were used on soft ground. This
view shows the St. Rollox works
and stone depot. Wagons are
being discharged from the high
level into the yards of various
coal traders. The locomotive 'St.
Rollox' is starting out with a
train of empty wagons. In the
distance are familiar features of
the Glasgow skyline.

The Station at Euston Square
London and Birmingham
    Railway
Artist: T. T. Bury
Engraver: J. Harris
Date: 1837
From: T. T. Bury, *The London and
    Birmingham Railroad*
Coloured Aquatint
Publisher: Ackermann, London

The building of Euston Station
gives an indication of the anxiety
of railway companies to locate
their stations as near to London
as possible. The approach involved the construction of a steep
gradient, crossing the Regent's
Canal, and the building of in-
numerable road bridges. The soft
clays of North London required
high retaining walls. Four lines
of track entered the train shed,
built by the Cubitt brothers, covering some ten thousand square
feet. No demolition was caused
by the construction of the station
(as was to happen later with St.
Pancras), but the engineering
costs of getting to a point so close
to Euston Road were considerable.

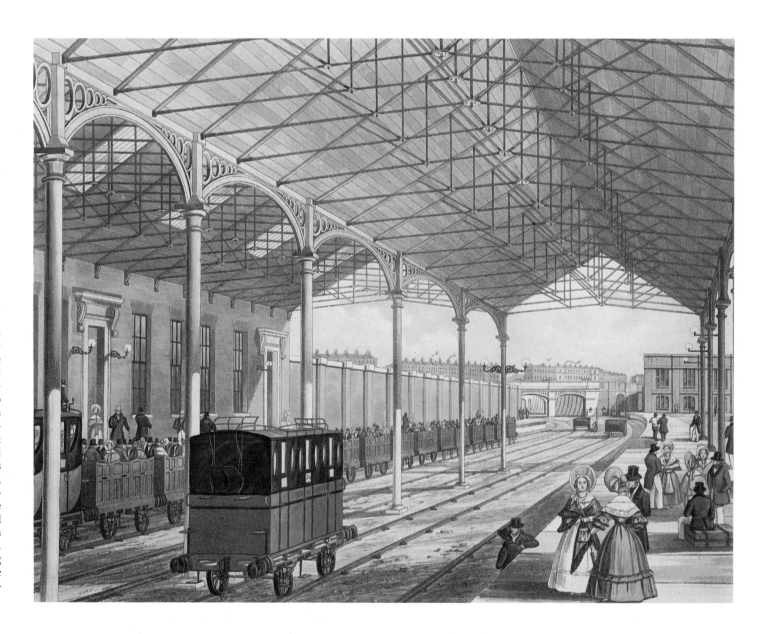

View taken from under the
  Hampstead Road Bridge,
  looking towards the Station at
  Euston Square
London and Birmingham
  Railway
Artist: T. T. Bury
Engraver: C. Hunt
Date: 1837
From: T. T. Bury, *The London and
  Birmingham Railroad*
Coloured Aquatint
Publisher: Ackermann, London

Bury gives an indication of the
scale of the retaining walls built
in the approaches to Euston. The
company originally intended to
make its London terminus at
Camden Town, but having built
Euston Station, found ways of
overcoming the one in seventy
incline up from the new terminus. From the opening of the first
section of the line to Box Moor in
1837 until 1844, when locomotives had enough power to man-
age the incline, coaches were
hauled up from Euston by a stationary engine and continuous
rope at Camden Town. In this
view the rope is clearly visible
between the tracks of the two up
lines, though locomotives did not
normally go down to Euston because of the steep gradient.

The Cowran Cut
Newcastle and Carlisle Railway
Artist: J. W. Carmichael
Engraver: L. Hassel
Date: 1836
From: J. Blackmore and J. W. Carmichael, *Views on the Newcastle and Carlisle Railway*
Black and White Engraving
Publisher: Currie & Bowman, Newcastle

Undertaken at the suggestion of the directors, Carmichael's twenty-three views were published with an introduction by John Blackmore at one guinea. The cutting is eight miles from Carlisle, nearly a mile long and is walled to a height of fourteen feet at the deepest point. It had originally been intended to dig a tunnel but loose sand and gushing springs made a cutting necessary. At the time it was the deepest cutting in England. The line was one of the earliest long routes to be approved, but was not opened until 1839, some ten years after approval was first given for the route, using horse traction.

The Depot at Hexham
Newcastle and Carlisle Railway
Artist: J. W. Carmichael
Engraver: J. Archer
Date: 1836
From: J. Blackmore and J. W. Carmichael, *Views on the Newcastle and Carlisle Railway*
Black and White Engraving
Publisher: Currie & Bowman, Newcastle

A busy station scene occupies the foreground yet the distant view of Hexham is unmistakable. The Abbey Church and Old Abbey dominate the horizon. A great deal of information is conveyed by the station scene: the 'Comet' locomotive waits without its tender while passenger and freight trains are prepared. Third-class passengers travel on the roof of first-class carriages. A variety of goods has been packed into low-sided trucks, and more are arriving. Considering its length (over sixty miles), the line was not as heavily used as the engraving would have us believe; in the late 1840s it carried about a quarter of a million passengers a year and its total receipts for passengers and freight were well under a hundred thousand pounds.

View Taken from the Bridge
    Over the Canal, Camden
    Town
London and Birmingham
    Railway
Artist: T. T. Bury
Engraver: N. Fielding
Date: 1837
From: T. T. Bury, *The London and
    Birmingham Railroad*
Coloured Aquatint
Publisher: Ackermann, London

In the third of Bury's views of the
London and Birmingham Railway, a train is being hauled up
from Euston to Camden Town
by the stationary engine. The
Canal Bridge, like many of the
bridges at the London end of the
line, shows complex iron decora-
tion. A railway policeman, in the
green livery of the company, is
sitting between the tracks, while
a train guard, with control of the
brakes, watches the continuous
rope.

Bridge Over the Canal Near
    Kings Langley
London and Birmingham
    Railway
Artist: T. T. Bury
Engraved by: J. Harris
Date: 1837
From: T. T. Bury, *The London and
    Birmingham Railroad*
Coloured Aquatint
Publisher: Ackermann, London

For nearly thirty miles the Grand
Junction Canal and the London
and Birmingham Railway ran
parallel to each other. On emerging from Watford Tunnel, the line
ran on an embankment nearly
three miles long broken by Nash
Mill Bridge over the canal. This
oblique bridge was made of iron
and consisted of six ribs forming
segmented arches of sixty-six
feet span. The width of the
bridge is explained by the fact
that the canal was in fact a
navigation, a widened and
deepened river bed, at this point.
The paper mill of Dickinson and
Longman was situated nearby,
and the industrial activity in the
foreground seems associated with
further river improvements.

The River Wall at Wylam Scars
Newcastle and Carlisle Railway
Artist: J. W. Carmichael
Engraver: H. Griffiths
Date: 1836
From: J. Blackmore and J. W.
    Carmichael, *Views on the
    Newcastle and Carlisle Railway*
Black and White Engraving
Publisher: Currie & Bowman,
    Newcastle

The river wall is on the south bank of the Tyne, some nine miles from Newcastle. The line was built on rubble quarried from the rocks above for about three-quarters of a mile. On the opposite bank is Wylam Colliery and Iron Works. The bridge was paid for by public subscription to give access to the works from the railway. The mixture of passengers and freight on the train seems typical of Carmichael's other views of the line.

View of the River Lea Bridge and Stratford Viaduct as now
constructing for the Eastern Counties Railway Company
From a drawing by: G. Harley
On Stone by: L. Haghe
Date: 1837
Coloured Lithograph
Lithographers: Day & Haghe, London

The Eastern Counties Railway, incorporated in 1836, was originally planned to run from London to Yarmouth but did not even reach Colchester until 1843. This slow progress was caused by weak financial support from a relatively poor part of England. The line is shown here in its very early days, only a few miles out of London, and before the line was opened.

The Entrance to the Tunnel at Watford
London and Birmingham Railway
Artist: T. T. Bury
Engraver: N. Fielding
Date: 1837
From: T. T. Bury, *The London and Birmingham Railroad*
Coloured Aquatint
Publisher: Ackermann, London

The train appears to be entering the tunnel on the wrong track, but within a few months of its opening the railway has become a matter of indifference to the figures in the foreground. Sheep may graze close to the edge of its precipitous cuttings. The line was expensively built by Robert Stephenson, who is said to have covered the route fifteen times in surveying it. Gradients rarely exceeded one in three hundred and curves were of a generous radius. Thus much of the line was in cuttings or on embankments and twenty thousand men were employed on it at its peak.

The Viaduct at Watford
London and Birmingham Railway
Artist: T. T. Bury
Engraved by: J. Harris
Date: 1837
From: T. T. Bury, *The London and Birmingham Railroad*
Coloured Aquatint
Publisher: Ackermann, London

The railway skirted Watford in a wide curve from the eastern to the northern side of the town on a long embankment about forty feet high, built of the spoils of Oxhey cutting and the approaches to Watford tunnel. At the centre of the three-quarter-mile embankment was a viaduct of five semi-circular arches. One of the arches was oblique, and under it was a turnpike whose gate is visible in the view. But for the opposition of powerful landowners in the direction of Cassiobury and Grove, the railway could have avoided the expensive embankments, viaducts and tunnels in the vicinity of Watford, saving many thousands of pounds.

ENTRANCE TO LOCOMOTIVE ENGINE HOUSE CAMDEN TOWN

The Entrance to the Locomotive
Engine House, Camden Town
London and Birmingham
Railway
Artist: J. C. Bourne
On Stone by: J. C. Bourne
Date: 1839
From: J. C. Bourne, *Drawings of
the London and Birmingham
Railway*
Black and White Lithograph
Publisher: Bourne & Ackermann,
London

Because of the gradient down to
Euston, the locomotives of the
London and Birmingham Railway were kept at Camden Town.
In the first really expensive and
comprehensive publication relat-
ing to a single line, John Cooke
Bourne produced thirty views to
accompany John Britton's descriptive account. In terms of the
technical information they incor-
porate, Bourne's views are more
accurate than those of his con-
temporaries. In the locomotive
emerging from the engine house,
Bourne shows how far locomotive design had evolved since
Shaw's Liverpool and Manchester locomotives. The boiler and
smokebox is now mounted rather
higher, with horizontally
mounted pistons beneath it, and
large spring buffers on the front
of the frame.

Euston Square Station
London and Birmingham Railway
Engraver: Samuel Williams
Date: 1840
From: Osborne's *London and Birmingham Railway Guide*
Black and White Steel Engraving
Publisher: E. C. & W. Osborne, Birmingham and London

Railway guides began to appear in the 1830s, to give passengers and
prospective travellers some running explanation of the line and how to
travel on it. These publications were cheap – usually between one and
five shillings – and while a few of the more expensive ones contained
good copper engravings, the cheaper ones had a few small woodcuts or
steel engravings. Although often crude, they make interesting compari-
sons with railway prints. Here, for example, is Osborne's equivalent of
Bury's Euston (Plate 25). A guard has just brought a train down from
Camden Town 'under gravity', controlling its speed with the brake
handle to the right of his perch on the leading carriage. Some of the
company's two hundred special constables (in top hats) are directing
and helping passengers from the train, while some of the hundred and
sixty company porters move the luggage. Gratuities were forbidden. A
cleaner sets about the carriages, while others can be seen on the far
platform. Although this scene is less elegant than Bury's, it says much
more about the organization and bustle of a station.

Primrose Hill Tunnel
London and Birmingham Railway
Artist: J. C. Bourne
Date: 1837
Watercolour

Situated between St. John's Wood and Finchley and not far from Chalk Farm, Primrose Hill Tunnel also appeared as a lithograph in Bourne's *Drawings of the London and Birmingham Railway*. Nearly twelve hundred yards in length it was the first long tunnel experienced by those taking their first train journey from Euston. This was recognized by John Britton in his introduction to Bourne's work: 'this subterranean channel ... usually excites strong anxieties and terrors in the timid mind.' But Britton explained reassuringly that thousands had passed through it without accident or injury in a couple of minutes. The Italianate style of the tunnel mouth was, according to F. W. Simms, 'selected as admitting bold features expressive of the strength by which Railway works should, it is presumed, be characterised.' (1838).

Knaresborough Viaduct
East and West Yorkshire
  Junction Railway
Artist: R. O. Hodgson
On Stone by: J. C. Bourne
Date: About 1850
Hand-Coloured Lithograph
Publisher: C. F. Cheffins, London

Although Bourne is best known for his works on the London and Birmingham and Great Western Railways, he occasionally produced single views of picturesque railway scenes. Quite when this view was executed is not clear: Bourne was associated with the railway architect, printer and publisher Charles Cheffins from the early 1840s and may have worked for him as an engineering draughtsman. Cheffins supervised and financed the publication of Bourne's *Great Western Railway*, but it is thought that Bourne ceased to be interested in British railway scenes after 1846, working in Russia with Charles Vignoles from about 1847. Knaresborough acquired two railways in the late 1840s: the Leeds and Thirsk and the East and West Yorkshire Junction, which aimed to join the former to the York, Newcastle and Berwick Railway. Approved in 1846, the line was not even partly opened until 1850, which makes this view one of the very last with which Bourne was associated.

Panorama of Camden Town Depot
London and Birmingham Railway
Artist: J. C. Bourne
On Stone by: J. C. Bourne
Date: 1839
From: J. C. Bourne, *Drawings of the London and Birmingham Railway*
Black and White Lithograph
Publisher: Bourne & Ackermann, London

This view, which contains a great deal of helpful detail, makes clear the arrangements at Camden. The twin chimneys are those of the two sixty horse-power marine stationary engines used to pull trains up from Euston, which is over the horizon beyond the chimneys. Locomotives are waiting for such trains. In the middle is the engine shed, which covered three-quarters of an acre and contained tanks in the roof to supply locomotives with water before their journey, as well as lathes, furnaces and anvils for repairing them. In the foreground is what Bourne calls an 'Eccentric for shifting rail' which makes clear how points worked. The whole complex at Camden Town covered thirty acres and included facilities for goods and cattle, warehouses and storerooms, coal yards and coke ovens.

Building the Stationary Engine House, Camden Town
London and Birmingham Railway
Artist: J. C. Bourne
On Stone by: J. C. Bourne
Date: 1839
From: J. C. Bourne, *Drawings of the London and Birmingham Railway*
Black and White Lithograph
Publishers: Bourne & Ackermann, London

The twin chimneys of Camden Town engine house were a major landmark of North London, being one hundred and thirty-two feet high. The engines themselves were in what Britton described as 'a large vaulted structure beneath the surface of the railway'. This is partly apparent in the deep excavation shown by Bourne in this view. Also incorporated in the engine house were the winding wheels for the continuous rope, the largest of which was twenty feet in diameter. The sixty horse-power engines were built by Mawdesly and Field.

Nottingham Railway Station
Midland Counties Railway
Artist: A. Parker
On Stone by: G. Hawkins Jnr.
Lithographers: Day & Haghe, London
Date: 1839
Coloured Lithograph
Publisher: W. Dearden, Nottingham

The first sixteen miles of the Midland Counties Railway, the section between Derby and Nottingham, were opened on 4 June 1839. This lithograph was published locally a month later. It shows a large crowd assembled for the departure of a train. Nottingham Castle dominates the background. The view gives the impression that the railway reached only the edge of town, because not only have townspeople come out *en famille* to see the spectacle, the rural gentry have also arrived on horseback: the 'two nations' of Disraeli's novel *Sybil* united to welcome the railway.

Train with Open Carriages full
of Passengers about to Enter a
Station
Artist: Unknown
Date: About 1840
Coloured Lithograph

This view is a complete mystery,
yet its quality makes it of great
interest. It is to be found in the
Elton Collection at Ironbridge,
and the late Sir Arthur Elton
considered it to be a view of the
Glasgow and Paisley Railway,
opened in 1839. There are some
clues in the six-wheeled locomotive and the open-sided carriages, both of which suggest the
Liverpool and Manchester Railway. The locomotive is about to
enter a train shed, while the
waiting travellers are segregated
– the expensive, coloured clothes
of the wealthier passengers are in
sharp contrast to the black mass
of poor people confined outside
the gates.

BUILDING RETAINING WALL &c NEAR PARK STREET, CAMDEN TOWN SEPT 17th 1836

Blasting Rocks at Linslade, Buckinghamshire
London and Birmingham Railway
Artist: J. C. Bourne
On Stone by: J. C. Bourne
Date: 1839
From: J. C. Bourne, *Drawings of the London and Birmingham Railway*
Black and White Lithograph
Publishers: Bourne & Ackermann, London

So anxious was Robert Stephenson to keep the London and Birmingham line as level and straight as possible, that at no point was the line more than three hundred feet above Camden Town Station or fifty feet above Birmingham Station. The highest point of the line was just over thirty miles from London, in Buckinghamshire. This view shows the line under construction between Leighton Buzzard and Bletchley, near Linslade tunnel. Rocks are being blasted to make a cutting through Jackdaw Hill. Curiously, one line is being built on stone and one on wooden sleepers, though these may have been temporary arrangements for the contractors' wagons.

Building a Retaining Wall near
  Park Street, Camden Town
London and Birmingham
  Railway
Artist: J. C. Bourne
On Stone by: J. C. Bourne
Date: 1839
From: J. C. Bourne, *Drawings of the London and Birmingham Railway*
Black and White Lithograph
Publishers: Bourne & Ackermann, London

Dickens described the building of the great cutting through Camden Town some ten years after the event in the serialized *Dombey and Son* (1846–8). 'Houses were knocked down; streets broken through and stopped; deep pits and trenches dug in the ground; enormous heaps of earth and clay thrown up; buildings that were undermined and shaking propped by great beams of wood . . . Everywhere were bridges that led nowhere; thoroughfares that were wholly impassable.' The view shows the high retaining walls built to hold back the soft clay subsoils of North London.

View of a Landslip near Dawlish
South Devon Railway
Artist: F. Jones
On Stone by: F. Jones
Lithographers: W. Spreat, Exeter
Date: 1852
Colour Lithograph
Publisher: Westcott, Dawlish

Most railway prints published after the end of the railway mania in 1847 concentrated on themes other than the railway itself, for example on great bridges or similar engineering feats. Here, however, is a view of the failure of railway engineering. The South Devon Railway's route from Exeter to Newton Abbot travelled for some miles along the coast and was damaged by storms on a number of occasions in its early years. In December 1852 this landslip occurred, and sections of track were washed away by the sea in February 1855 and in 1873. On the occasion of this view the line was blocked by a cliff fall so severe that for a few days coaches again ran on the road from Dawlish to Teignmouth.

Chirk Viaduct
Shrewsbury and Chester
     Railway
Artist: G. Pickering
On Stone by: George Hawkins Jnr.
Lithographers: Day & Son
Date: 1848
Coloured Lithograph
Publisher: Catherall, Chester

Chirk, between Oswestry and Llangollen, is one of the few places where the greatest feats of different transport technologies coincide. The Holyhead Road, engineered to high specifications by Telford in the second and third decades of the nineteenth century, was complemented by his fine canal aqueduct, and then in the 1840s by Chirk Viaduct on the Shrewsbury and Chester Railway. The viaduct was nearly eight hundred and fifty feet long, one hundred feet high. It consisted of twelve stone arches of forty-five feet in span, and two timber arches of one hundred and twenty feet each. In this view, the aqueduct can be seen through the arches of the railway viaduct.

Blisworth Cutting
London and Birmingham Railway
Artist: J. C. Bourne
On Stone by: J. C. Bourne
Date: 1839
From: J. C. Bourne, *Drawings of the London and Birmingham Railway*
Black and White Lithograph
Publishers: Bourne & Ackermann, London

Blisworth Cutting, between Wolverton and Rugby, was at the point where the London and Birmingham passed close to Northampton. The cutting was one and a half miles long and in places the track was sixty feet below the surface. The quantity of material excavated from it was estimated at one million cubic yards. In this view, Bourne makes what must then have been a fresh scar across the countryside appear graceful with its gentle curve and elegant bridge.

Tring Cutting
London and Birmingham
   Railway
Artist: J. C. Bourne
On Stone by: J. C. Bourne
Date: 1839
From: J. C. Bourne, *Drawings of the London and Birmingham Railway*
Black and White Lithograph
Publishers: Bourne & Ackermann, London

Bourne's Tring Cutting is perhaps the only early railway print to give an impression of the vast amounts of labour and the primitiveness of the technology used to remould the landscape. Leonardo da Vinci drew canals being excavated in much the same way because labour was the cheap ingredient in civil engineering in both the sixteenth and the nineteenth centuries. The London and Croydon Railway, for example, cost five thousand pounds per mile to build yet the labour cost was only two hundred and sixty pounds per mile. The horse-runs illustrated here were used to raise soil out of cuttings and to lift it onto embankments. The horse drew a rope which ran through two pulleys to a wheelbarrow, guided up sloping boards by a labourer. There were forty horse-runs in the cutting, yet only one life was lost through barrows falling onto their guides. The line's engineer designed a moving platform to replace the barrow and labourer, but the navvies destroyed it according to John Britton, considering it 'designed to lessen their labour and wages'.

The Atmospheric Railway at Dawlish
South Devon Railway
Artist: Nicholas Condy
Date: 1848
Watercolour

Views of atmospheric railways are so rare that this watercolour has been included to give an impression of it. The Italianate engine house produced the vacuum in the tube between the tracks, while the other tubes presumably conducted the vacuum to other sections of track some distance away. The continuous flap valve is clearly visible; it consisted of leather strengthened with iron. The advantages of the system were its quiet running, smooth acceleration and deceleration, and freedom from smoke and steam. The lightness of trains without locomotives enabled some savings to be made in bridge construction. But the disadvantages lay in the weakness of pumping engines and the impossibility of keeping a good seal on the continuous flap valve. This inefficiency caused the scrapping of the Exeter–Newton Abbot section; some of the tubes are visible today as drains on nearby beaches.

The Viaduct at Ivy Bridge, Devon
South Devon Railway
Artist: Unknown
Date: About 1848
Coloured Lithograph
Publisher: O. Angel or Spreat, Exeter

The South Devon Railway was famous for Brunel's abortive atmospheric experiment, and distinguished architecturally by a number of timber viaducts built to Brunel's designs at Slade, Glazebrook and Ivybridge. All three appeared in contemporary prints by several artists, and used the same structure of slender masonry piers supporting a timber frame. Because the line was designed with the single-track, light, atmospherically propelled trains in mind, the viaducts had to be strengthened when heavy steam locomotives were introduced. They were demolished in the 1890s when a second track was built.

Harrow on the Hill
London and Birmingham
  Railway
Artist: I. Wrightson
Engraver: Probably W. Radclyffe
Date: 1839
From: T. Roscoe, *History of the
  London and Birmingham Railway*
Copper Engraving
Publisher: Tilt, London

Among the mass-produced and
cheap guides to major routes,
those published by Thomas Roscoe included high quality, small
engravings. This distinguished
Roscoe's from the majority of
guides, whose standards of illustration were low, limited mainly
to minute woodcuts. In this view
of Harrow on the Hill a less
familiar location on the line is
treated well. Harrow Station was
an intermediate station, a mile
from the town. Second-class
trains stopped at such stations
for a few minutes only, while
first-class and mail trains passed
through. Yet Harrow Station
had a water cistern for locomotives, an office, a waiting room, a
clerk and porters.

Berkhampstead Station
London and Birmingham
  Railway
Artist: G. Dodgson
Engraver: E. Radclyffe
Date: 1839
From: T. Roscoe, *History of the
  London and Birmingham Railway*
Copper Engraving
Publisher: Tilt, London

Berkhampstead was another intermediate station, twenty-eight miles from Euston. It was built of brick with stone facings in the Gothic style to blend into the surroundings. The engravers of Roscoe's Guides seem concerned, as do most railway lithographers, to make the railway seem a natural part of an unchanging scene despite its novelty. The canal and village traffic continues unaffected by the railway and passengers wander informally across the tracks to meet an incoming train. Although small and printed in very large numbers, guide illustrations should not be overlooked in the study of the early railway age. The artist of this view collaborated with H. Belcher to produce *Illustrations of the Scenery on the Line of the Whitby and Pickering Railway* (1836).

The Goods Shed at Bristol
Great Western Railway
Artist: J. C. Bourne
On Stone by: J. C. Bourne
Date: 1846
From: J. C. Bourne, *History and Description of the Great Western Railway*
Coloured Lithograph
Publisher: Bogue, London

Whereas Bourne made drawings of the London and Birmingham Railway years before its opening, his studies of the Great Western were made nearly five years after its completion, when Bristol was already connected to Exeter and Birmingham. The decision to use a gauge of seven feet on the Great Western was a result of Brunel's belief that more powerful and faster locomotives could be used while carriages would be more comfortable. The standard gauge of four feet eight and a half inches was only a convention, and Brunel did not think in conventional terms, a fact demonstrated in such ventures as the Great Eastern Steamship and the South Devon Atmospheric Railway. Railway companies were private commercial organizations and were not concerned with a national network, at least until 1844 when the broad gauge reached Gloucester, already linked to Birmingham on standard gauge. In this view broad-gauge wagons and all the equipment of a goods depot are visible.

Bristol Station
Great Western Railway
Artist: J. C. Bourne
On Stone by: J. C. Bourne
Date: 1846
From: J. C. Bourne, *History and Description of the Great Western Railway*
Coloured Lithograph
Publisher: Bogue, London

The terminus of the Great Western Railway at Bristol was the grandest of all the company's buildings. It was certainly the only station roof to be built to resemble a banqueting hall of the Tudor period, complete with imitation hammerbeams. As in most stations, it seems to have been customary to cover sleepers with earth to create as level a surface as possible between the tracks. A six-wheeled express locomotive of the massive proportions possible only on the Great Western is visible; all the rolling stock seems oddly proportioned as a result of the broad gauge. By 1848 there was some two hundred and fifty miles of broad-gauge railway in operation.

The Working Shaft, Kilsby Tunnel
London and Birmingham Railway
Artist: J. C. Bourne
On Stone by: J. C. Bourne
Date: 1839
From: J. C. Bourne, *Drawings of the London and Birmingham Railway*
Black and White Lithograph
Publisher: Bourne & Ackermann, London

Kilsby Tunnel presented Robert Stephenson with by far his greatest problem in the construction of the London and Birmingham Railway. It was two thousand four hundred yards long, the longest railway tunnel to be built at that time, and it passed through underground springs and quicksands not revealed by preliminary surveys. The tunnel claimed twenty-six lives in its four-year construction and cost five times as much per foot as the rest of the line. Stephenson originally planned eight working shafts but had to double this number. Only after nine months of pumping nearly two thousand gallons of water a minute did the shafts become workable, and the tunnel was finished under Stephenson's personal supervision with continuous day and night shiftwork.

A View of the London and Croydon Railway from the Deep Cutting
   made through the Hill at New Cross, looking towards the Greenwich
   Railway
Artist: E. Duncan
On Stone by: E. Duncan
Lithographers: Day & Haghe, London
Date: 1838
Tinted Lithograph
Publisher: Ackermann, London

Opened in 1839, the London and Croydon Railway experimented in
1846–7 with the atmospheric system patented by Samuda and Clegg
but quickly abandoned it. Built with two tracks, the line was to have
used the atmospheric system on a third. Just over half a million cubic
yards of material were removed from the seventy-foot-deep cutting
shown in this view. In the distance the long viaduct of the London and
Greenwich Railway is visible. The two companies shared part of this,
which perhaps explains why the train in the view is on the wrong track:
the London and Greenwich had reversed the conventional arrangements of up and down lines.

View of New Street Bridge, Belper, looking South
North Midland Railway
Artist: S. Russell
On Zinc by: S. Russell
Lithographers: Day & Haghe, London
Date: 1840
Zincograph

S. Russell was one of the better of the little-known artist/lithographers. He seems to have had an eye for the texture of stone and in this view he shows how a skew bridge requires complex stone shapes to produce a symmetrical appearance. The bridge was built by Joseph Turner of Wingfield. This view is a zincograph, that is, an experimental attempt to print in colour. Hullmandel printed in colour from zinc plates in 1840, but Thomas Shotter Boys is credited with the invention of chromolithography in 1839. The London partnership of William Day and Louis Haghe is best known for its lithographs, produced between 1833 and 1851, but it employed a large staff of lithographic artists and experimented with colour printing in around 1840. This is one of its successes, striking in tone and clarity, although Russell clearly kept the subject matter simple and made it easy to align the sequence of colour printings by using the outline of the bridge.

The Bridge Under the Cromford Canal at Bull Bridge
North Midland Railway
Artist: S. Russell
On Stone by: S. Russell
Lithographers: Day & Haghe, London
Date: 1840
Coloured Lithograph

The North Midland Railway was incorporated in 1836, opened in 1840, and was part of the merger of companies that became the Midland Railway in 1844. It ran from Derby to Leeds. In this view canal, road and rail intersect. Two navvies have uncovered the chairs and sleepers to make some repairs. Russell seems to be making the point that the railway is just one more transport medium alongside its older rivals. Although it is possible to claim that canals and roads flourished where they acted as feeders to railheads, the railways caused great damage to the commercial viability of both.

The Railway Station at Wellington, Shropshire
Shrewsbury and Birmingham Railway
Artist: C. J. Greenwood
On Stone by: R. Groom
Lithographers: C. Moody, London
Date: July 1849
Black and White Lithograph
Publisher: J. Houlston, Wellington

The Shrewsbury and Birmingham Railway was opened in 1849, and amalgamated with the Great Western Railway in 1854. The chief engineer of the line was Robert Stephenson. Parliamentary approval in 1846 allowed for a branch to Coalbrookdale, the cradle of world industrialization. The view itself is typical of hundreds published locally to commemorate the arrival of the railway in a small country town. The passenger and freight stations are on opposite sides of the line. The approach of a train stimulated as much interest in small boys in 1849 as it does today.

Rock Cutting at Bishopton
Glasgow, Paisley and Greenock Railway
Artist: William McKenzie
Lithographers: Maclure & MacDonald
Date: March 1841
Coloured Lithograph
Publishers: Maclure & MacDonald

This company was authorized in 1837 to build a twenty-two-mile line from Glasgow to Greenock. The first seven miles, from Glasgow to Paisley, were opened in 1839 and were the joint property of the company and of the Glasgow, Paisley, Kilmarnock and Ayr Railway. The rest of the line, from Paisley to Greenock was not opened until 1841 because of difficulties encountered in making tunnels and cuttings through hard rock. As many as a thousand men were employed on this work, and the view shows the difficult terrain through which a seventy-foot-deep cutting was driven near Bishopton.

Bangor
Chester and Holyhead Railway
Artist: A.Y.S.
On Stone by: T. Picken
Lithographers: Day & Son
Date: About 1850
Coloured Lithograph
Publisher: G. Humphreys

This charming view of Bangor was drawn on stone by Thomas Picken, one of a number of obviously talented lithographers whose names appear occasionally on individually published views of lines in different parts of the country. Picken is known to have helped produce another view of Bangor and one of Bath Ford on the Great Western Railway. In this view the railway has blended unobtrusively into the hillside above Bangor. The line is already elevated in its approach to the Menai Tubular Bridge.

Chepstow Bridge Over the River Wye
South Wales Railway
Artist: W. Richardson
On Stone by: W. Richardson
Lithographers: Day & Haghe
Date: 1851
Coloured Lithograph
Publisher: R. Taylor, Chepstow

Chepstow Bridge was the last and most difficult link in the joining of South Wales to the growing rail network. The Taff Vale Railway had been opened as early as 1841, but there was no rail connection between the coalfields and England until the South Wales Railway was built, joining coastal towns to Gloucester in 1851. The crossing of the Wye at Chepstow presented particular difficulties, because one bank was a cliff and because of the large tidal rise and fall. These rendered a wooden structure impossible so Brunel designed an iron bridge that was light yet high enough to carry the railway well above the river. The result, shown in this view, was a compromise: it was partly a suspension bridge but made use of the strength of iron tubes. River shipping could pass beneath, even at high tide.

Swinton Station
North Midland Railway
Artist: Unknown
Date: About 1840
Tinted Lithograph
Publisher: Unknown

Although the artist and lithographer remain a mystery, this may have been a proof or a limited edition for the perusal of the directors or a local publisher. Swinton was an intermediate station on the North Midland line between Rotherham and Barnsley, yet it justified the construction of this fine neo-classical structure, which looks rather more like a lodge in the grounds of a country mansion than a railway station.

Tunbridge Wells Station
South Eastern Railway
Artist: J. C. Bourne
On Stone by: J. C. Bourne
Date: Mid-1840s
Tinted Lithograph

This fine view of a small country station is Bourne at his best. The work on the Great Western Railway had clearly influenced him as the gauge looks somewhat broader than standard. Hand shunting by railway staff was quite commonplace: whole trains were pushed by porters, carriage by carriage, to the winding rope outside Euston. In this view a train of carriages and wagons is being assembled in the foreground, while a carriage is being moved by three men from another platform. A small turntable is situated at the end of the main platform to help other marshalling activities.

Ely Cathedral
Eastern Counties Railway
Artist: Attributed to E. Duncan
Date. About 1850
Watercolour

Edward Duncan began his career as an aquatint engraver for Robert Havell, becoming well known for coastal and river scenes. He may have produced the view of the London and Croydon Railway on Plate 56. In this watercolour, a train is approaching a level crossing on the Newmarket Road before entering Ely Station. A barge travels up the River Ouse and the Cathedral towers above.

Willington Dean Viaduct
Newcastle, North Shields and
    Tynemouth Railway
Artist: T. M. Richardson
On Stone by: T. M. Richardson
Lithographers: A. Ducote, London
Date: 1838
Tinted Lithograph
Publishers: McLean, London;
    Loraine, Newcastle

Thomas Miles Richardson made lithographs of both Willington Dean and Ouse Burn Viaducts on the Newcastle, North Shields and Tynemouth Railway. The line was opened in 1839 and became part of the Newcastle and Berwick Railway in 1847. Both viaducts were famous for their unorthodox construction: they were built of laminated timber on masonry piers, like those on the South Devon Railway, only on a bigger scale. Willington Dean had seven spans of one hundred and twenty feet, was a thousand and fifty feet in length and over eighty feet high. Each span consisted of three ribs of deal with a timber frame above to carry the track. Although it looks fragile to modern eyes, timber was a logical raw material to use in the early days when trains were light and iron expensive. Moreover, timber bridges kept down the initial cost of building a line, important to a new company. Timber could always be replaced with other materials when maintenance became necessary.

Defford Bridge on the River
   Avon
Birmingham and Gloucester
   Railway
Artist: Edwin Dolby
On Stone by: Clerk & Co., London
Date: 1839
Black and White Lithograph
Publisher: R. A. Sprigg, London

Authorized in 1836, this fifty-mile line was built by 1840 to provide Birmingham with direct access to the West Country, avoiding the journey via London. It was built to Stephenson's standard gauge, which helped confine the broad gauge to the south and west. The railway achieved two unusual firsts: it was the earliest line to be approved by Parliament at the first attempt; and it was the first line to use printed tickets, in 1845. This view by Edwin Dolby, who is associated with other illustrations of the line, shows the Defford Bridge over the River Avon in Worcestershire. Its spans were fifty-eight feet, and its height above water was twenty-eight feet.

The Lickey Inclined Plane
Birmingham and Gloucester Railway
Artist: Edwin Dolby
On Stone by: Clerk & Co., London
Date: June 1840
Black and White Lithograph

The Birmingham and Gloucester Railway was opened in 1840, and, according to Edward Baker, was noteworthy for a number of reasons. It was on this line that Brunel did his first surveying; like the Stockton and Darlington, it was financed by Quakers; and it had to skirt important towns to avoid expense. But its most significant feature was the Lickey Incline, a two-mile bank near Bromsgrove with a gradient of one in thirty-seven. Brunel and Stephenson declared it impossible to ascend with locomotives, so Captain Moorsom, the line's engineer, was forced to order bogie engines from Norris of Philadelphia. These could ascend at maximum speeds of around nine miles per hour by virtue of their small driving wheels. This view shows one such locomotive on a steep section of the incline with a train of a total weight of seventy-four tons. The track is carried on longitudinal sleepers.

Viaduct Over the Valley of the Weaver
Chester and Crewe Railway
Artist: G. Pickering
On Stone by: J. C. Bourne
Lithographers: C. F. Cheffins, London
Date: Early 1840s
Tinted Lithograph
Publishers: Evans & Ducker, Chester; Cheffins, London

This view with its unconventional composition – the subject is partly obscured rather than framed by the trees – shows the type of viaduct that became typical later in the nineteenth century. Wood was used occasionally, iron in exceptional circumstances, but brick and stone of local origin were the materials for most large bridges and viaducts. At the time Bourne was probably working for Cheffins – who dedicated this view to George Stephenson – in his printing and publishing offices.

Warrington
Grand Junction Railway
Artist: Unknown
Engraver: W. Radclyffe
Date: 1839
From: T. Roscoe, *The Book of the Grand Junction Railway*
Copper Engraving
Publisher: Orr & Company, London

Roscoe made use of four artists, Cox, Bentley, Dodgson and Radclyffe for the few tiny illustrations that appeared with his guides. This vignette, which is slightly enlarged, is a rare example of an illustration in which the railway features prominently. It shows a train leaving Warrington on the stone bridge over the Mersey, with a crew of permanent way workers in attendance. In Roscoe's own words, 'the town, as it is approached through the pleasant fields on each side of the line, with its tall chimnies sending forth columns of smoke, the embattled towers of its churches and the extent to which it appears to spread itself out, possesses the traveller with a sense of its great wealth and consequence.'

Sonning Cutting
Great Western Railway
Artist: J. C. Bourne
On Stone by: J. C. Bourne
Date: 1846
From: J. C. Bourne, *History and Description of the Great Western Railway*
Black and White Lithograph
Publisher: Bogue, London

This view shows what is thought to be Brunel's first timber bridge, an overbridge to carry a road across Sonning Cutting, built in 1840. It is perhaps surprising that the architect of sophisticated iron structures such as those at Chepstow and Saltash should have built in wood, but it proved strong and durable. Also of interest in this view are the longitudinal sleepers with intermittent cross-sleepers supported on piles which Brunel used on the Great Western. Longitudinal sleepers were used until the end of the broad gauge in 1892.

Victoria Station, Hunt's Bank,
  Manchester
Manchester and Leeds Railway
Artist: A. F. Tait
On Stone by: A. F. Tait
Lithographers: Day & Haghe,
  London
Date: 1845
From: A. F. Tait and E.
  Butterworth, *Views on the
  Manchester and Leeds Railway*
Black and White Lithograph
Publishers: Bradshaw &
  Blacklock, Manchester

This view is taken from Tait's best-known work, his nineteen *Views on the Manchester and Leeds Railway*, published in 1845 with an introduction by Edwin Butterworth. Nearly all the views in this book are large landscapes seen from the railway, or containing the railway as a distant feature, reflecting its complete acceptance by this time. However, this view of Victoria Station is the one great exception: it shows the interior of the station jointly built by the Manchester and Leeds and the Liverpool and Manchester Railways in 1844. The train shed, designed by George Stephenson, covered eighty thousand square feet, and was the largest at that time.

Pangbourne Station
Great Western Railway
Artist: J. C. Bourne
On Stone by: J. C. Bourne
Date: 1846
From: J. C. Bourne, *History and Description of the Great Western Railway*
Black and White Lithograph
Publisher: Bogue, London

In general, two architectural styles were most favoured by railway companies: a sort of Tudor/Jacobean of which this is an example, and a villa-like Italianate style. As a very broad generalization, the former style was favoured in small rural stations and the latter in small urban stations, but there are many exceptions. Pangbourne Station has a charming little booking office and a small shelter on the opposite platform. Britain seems to have been the only country to have given its passengers carriage-height platforms from the start of railway development in the nineteenth century.

The Engine House, Swindon
Great Western Railway
Artist: J. C. Bourne
On Stone by: J. C. Bourne
Date: 1846
From: J. C. Bourne, *History and Description of the Great Western Railway*
Black and White Lithograph
Publisher: Bogue, London

As a suitable half-way point between London and Bristol, Swindon developed into the Great Western Railway's main repair workshop and depot. When Bourne saw it, the engine house was two hundred and ninety feet by one hundred and forty, divided by two rows of columns into three sections. The locomotives stood in stalls to either side of a central pit, along which ran a moving platform. Thirty-six locomotives could be 'stabled' in this way for light repairs or maintenance. The Swindon Works grew rapidly in size in the late 1840s, covering over fourteen acres in 1849. When the French current affairs periodical *Magasin Pittoresque* produced an article and illustrations of it in 1852, Swindon Works was considered one of the foremost engineering workshops in Europe.

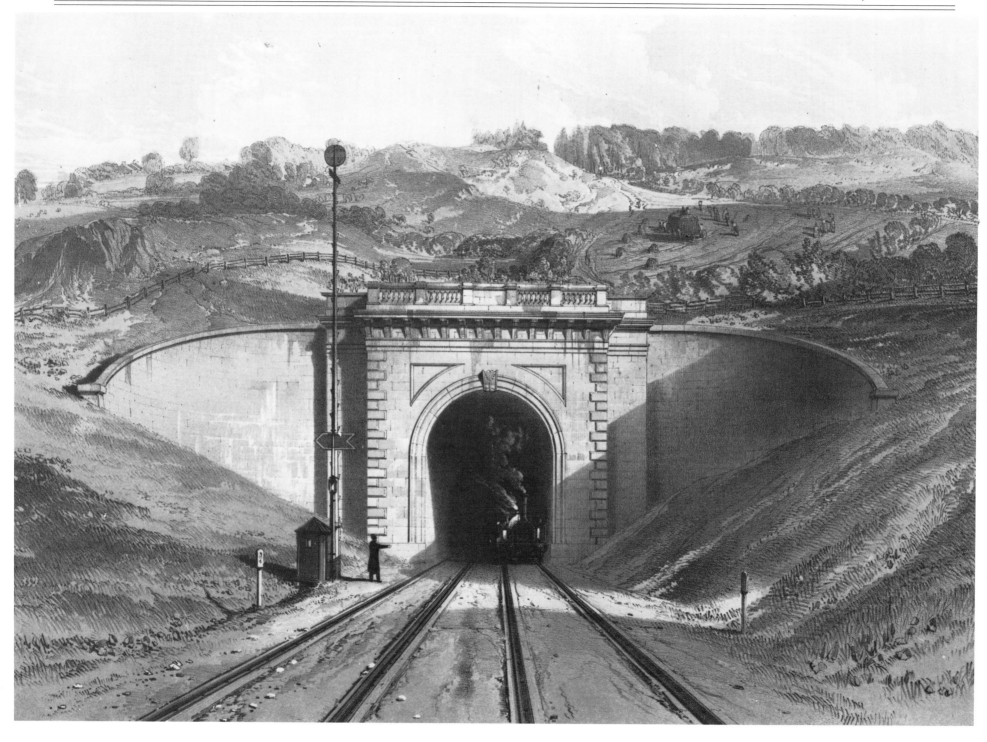

Box Tunnel, West Front
Great Western Railway
Artist: J. C. Bourne
On Stone by: J. C. Bourne
Date: 1846
From: J. C. Bourne, *History and Description of the Great Western Railway*
Black and White Lithograph
Publisher: Bogue, London

Box Tunnel, near Bath, was nearly two miles long, the longest in the world at that time. The solid and somewhat decorated appearance of the west front was intended to advertise the reliability of the railway and perhaps to abate the fears of those entering it. The length of tunnels like this gave rise to a signalling problem, hence the manned signal post visible in the view. In 1847 the two mouths of Box Tunnel were connected by telegraph so that the entry and exit of a train could be completed before another was allowed onto the section. The practice spread to other long tunnels around the mid-century.

West Entrance to Box Tunnel
Great Western Railway
Engraver: J. Shury
Date: About 1840

This small illustration from a railway guide makes an interesting comparison with Bourne's much larger lithograph of the same subject (Plate 75). The hollowed-out spaces between the cross-sleepers were perhaps for drainage purposes.

Kelston Bridge Near Bath
Great Western Railway
Artist: L. Haghe
On Stone by: L. Haghe
Lithographers: Lavars & Ackland, Bristol
Date: 1840
From: W. W. Young and L. Haghe, *Illustrations of the Great Western and Bristol and Exeter Railways*
Black and White Lithograph
Publishers: Hamilton, Adams & Co., London; Lavars & Ackland, Bristol

Haghe's views of the Great Western are less accurate and less graceful than Bourne's but they concentrate more on the railway itself, often featuring it in the foreground. This view offends all landscape conventions by placing a train between the spectator and the alleged subject. All attention that might have gone to the distant bridge is focused on the nonchalant personnel of the train and the curiously stylized locomotive. Nevertheless, the view has considerable charm, and the railway looks at home in the landscape despite its effect on the perspective of Kelston Bridge.

Bath Station
Great Western Railway
Artist: J. C. Bourne
On Stone by: J. C. Bourne
Date: 1846
From: J. C. Bourne, *History and Description of the Great Western Railway*
Black and White Lithograph
Publisher: Bogue, London

This view of rolling stock under the fine roof of Bath Station shows how little use the Great Western Railway made of the broad gauge. The wheels seem to have determined the width of coaches and wagons alike, so that in practice they were scarcely wider than those on standard-gauge railways where the body-work overhung either side of the track. Once the broad gauge had been prevented from spreading into the Midlands by Government restrictions in 1845, the number of points where the gauges met increased and it was only a question of time before the Great Western would have to conform. Thus it can hardly be blamed for not investing a great deal in new rolling stock from, say, 1870. The rolling stock in this view looks so low and square as to be ungainly.

The Interior of the Great Western Railway Station, Bristol
Great Western Railway
Artist: S. C. Jones
On Stone by: G. Hawkins Jnr.
Date: Early 1840s
Black and White Lithograph
Publisher: Davey, Bristol

This view makes an interesting comparison with Bourne's lithograph of the same train shed looking in the other direction (Plate 54). George Hawkins the Younger was responsible for a number of railway prints (see Plates 41 and 45) and is particularly associated with the Midland Counties Railway. Although this view is almost certainly earlier than Bourne's, the composition is almost identical, with an entire train seen on the right-hand platform, and much of the detail of the roof and platforms is similar. However, here we see a solution to the problem of moving rolling stock in the confined space of a train shed: in the foreground is a sliding platform operated by a hand winch, rather similar to the device in the centre of Swindon engine house (see Plate 74), enabling trains to be assembled behind a locomotive on the outward platform.

Edge Hill Station
London and North Western Railway
Artist: A. F. Tait
On Stone by: A. F. Tait
Date: 1848
Tinted Lithograph
Publishers: Bradshaw & Blacklock, Manchester

This view forms part of a set of fifteen relatively unknown lithographs of the London and North Western Railway. Perhaps the most powerful of all the railway companies by 1850, the London and North Western was an amalgamation of the companies that made up the trunk route from London to Liverpool, plus branches. It claimed four hundred and twenty-eight miles in operation in 1848. Tait's views cover the section from Liverpool to Stafford only, but the fifteen views in the National Railway Museum in York may not be the complete set. It seems probable that Bradshaw and Blacklock had intended to do for the London and North Western what Bourne had done for the Great Western, but that the bursting of the bubble of railway speculation in 1847 prevented Tait's views from being published as a volume. In this view crowds wait at Edge Hill Station, Liverpool.

Crewe Station
London and North Western
  Railway
Artist: A. F. Tait
On Stone by: A. F. Tait
Date: 1848
Tinted Lithograph
Publishers: Bradshaw &
  Blacklock, Manchester

Even before 1848, Crewe was an important junction for Manchester, Merseyside, Chester and Birmingham. In this view Tait gives much detail of the workings of a through station. It is hard to believe that the area between the tracks was paved in the manner indicated here: bricks or stone slabs would have lifted and cracked with the vibration caused by trains. Once again, passengers are seen wandering nonchalantly across the tracks. The platform is covered by a Regency-style roof. The milk churns visible on the platform end are a reminder of the new urban food supply made possible by the railway.

Crewe Station
London and North Western
    Railway
Artist: A. F. Tait
On Stone by: A. F. Tait
Date: 1848
Tinted Lithograph
Publishers: Bradshaw &
    Blacklock, Manchester

Looking in the opposite direction
to the previous view, Tait here
shows the station approaches to
Crewe. Notable features are the
lack of signals, the inspection pit
between the tracks next to the
platform and the water cistern on
the extreme right. Although Tait
was born near Liverpool in 1819,
his reputation was established in
America where he went to live in
1850. He died in 1905 renowned
as a painter of sporting scenes
and animals. His most popular
works were lithographs published by Currier and Ives. He
does not seem to have returned
to the railway as a subject after
1848.

Olive Mount
London and North Western
  Railway
Artist: A. F. Tait
On Stone by: A. F. Tait
Date: 1848
Tinted Lithograph
Publishers: Bradshaw &
  Blacklock, Manchester

On revisiting the Olive Mount cutting some sixteen years after Shaw (see Plate 19), Tait found it a less bleak place. Some vegetation was sprouting from the vertical rock walls, and it was being widened, or perhaps quarried, as shaped stone slabs are here being loaded onto flat trucks. Tait was clearly less impressed with the cragginess and depth of the cutting than Bury and Shaw, who were more concerned to stress the engineering accomplishment of the cutting. Sunlight and age had mellowed it to look almost natural to Tait.

Dawlish From the Line of the South Devon Railway
South Devon Railway
Artist: W. Dawson
On Stone by: W. Dawson
Date: 1848
Coloured Lithograph
Publisher: W. Spreat, Exeter

One of a set of six coloured lithographs of the South Devon Railway made in August and October 1848, this was the only one to show the atmospheric railway in any detail. Unfortunately, Dawson chose almost exactly the same spot as Condy for his watercolour (see Plate 49) and these two are the best record available of the system. Both show the same engine house and the vacuum tubes. The tube with the flap valve between the tracks was the train tube, while the others presumably conducted the vacuum to other sections of track. What Brunel was trying to do in principle – i.e. move several trains by a constant power source off the track – is what overhead electric traction accomplishes today. Brunel was, as usual, ahead of contemporary technology and materials in his thinking. The fact that several railway companies were tempted to use the atmospheric system was an indirect result of exaggerated claims made for it, and reflects belief in the almost magical powers of engineers. James Pim, in letters to wealthy peers written in 1841, proposed speeds of two hundred to a thousand miles per hour and the hiring out of stationary engines, when trains were not running, for land drainage, sawing wood and grinding oats.

Teignmouth in Broad Gauge Days
South Devon Railway
Artist: Unknown
Date: About 1850
Black and White Lithograph
Publisher: Unknown

This view of a train approaching Teignmouth from Dawlish was made after the atmospheric railway was abandoned, and steam was introduced on the South Devon Railway. Single-tracked until late in the nineteenth century, the line was one of the most spectacular built in Britain, following the shore-line from Dawlish Warren to Teignmouth.

Crumlin Viaduct on the Taff Vale Extension of the West Midland
  Railway
Artist: H. J. Cooke
Lithographers: Maclure, MacDonald & MacGregor
Date: 1860
Coloured Lithograph

Although most South Wales coal was carried to ports by local railways such as the Taff Vale and then shipped out, there was a strong inducement for railway companies to penetrate the area from the Midlands. One result of this was Crumlin Viaduct, built on a line from the Newport, Abergavenny and Hereford Railway at Pontypool westwards to the Taff Vale line at Quaker's Yard. The line was to become part of the West Midland Railway in 1860 which was in turn absorbed by the Great Western Railway in 1863. Nearly a third of a mile long and two hundred feet high, Crumlin Viaduct was one of the last to inspire several lithographs. It was built entirely of iron, and was opened after exhaustive tests in June 1857. Some of its girders weighed fifty tons.

Britannia Tubular Bridge, Platform and Construction of Tubes
Chester and Holyhead Railway
Artist: G. Hawkins
On Stone by: G. Hawkins
Lithographers: Day & Son
Date: 1849
From: E. Clark, *The Britannia and Conway Tubular Bridges*
Tinted Lithograph
Publisher: Russell, London

The iron tubes for the Britannia Bridge were built on a specially constructed platform on a bank adjacent to the site. When completed the first tube was floated into position and lifted up the piers to the appropriate level. So large was the undertaking that separate contractors were engaged for the tubes, the hydraulic presses to lift the tubes, and the masonry and scaffolding. Each tube over water was four hundred and sixty feet long, thirty feet deep and nearly fifteen feet wide. As the plates were up to three-quarters of an inch thick, each tube weighed one thousand eight hundred tons. The first tube was successfully locked in position on 20 June 1849, a feat celebrated by Brunel and Stephenson with champagne on top of the tube.

Britannia Tubular Bridge Over the Menai Straits
Chester and Holyhead Railway
Artist: G. Hawkins
On Stone by: G. Hawkins
Lithographers: Day & Son
Date: 1848
From: E. Clark, *The Britannia and Conway Tubular Bridges*
Tinted Lithograph
Publisher: Russell, London

Robert Stephenson first projected a line from Chester to Holyhead in 1836, but no company would back such a vast undertaking. He therefore formed a company of his own and gained parliamentary approval for the line in 1844. The problem of crossing the Menai Straits was exacerbated by the Admiralty's concern that the Straits should remain navigable to tall-masted sailing ships. After building a number of models, Stephenson finally settled on a tubular design, also used in the Conway Bridge. In this view the embankments and piers are seen under construction.

Britannia Tubular Bridge Over
the Menai Straits, Showing
the Floating of the Second
Tube, 3 December 1849
Chester and Holyhead Railway
Artist: G. Hawkins
On Stone by: G. Hawkins
Lithographers: Day & Son
Date: 1849
From: E. Clark, *The Britannia and
Conway Tubular Bridges*
Tinted Lithograph
Publisher: Russell, London

Eight pontoons were used to float
the tubes out into the river, and
these displaced a total of two
thousand seven hundred and
fifty tons. It took fifty-six minutes
to float the second tube out into
position, and a further seventeen
days to raise it into position. The
architectural structure of the
piers was designed by Francis
Thompson with a suspension
bridge in mind, as can be seen by
the cable ports at the top of each
pier.

Britannia Tubular Bridge Over
  the Menai Straits
Chester and Holyhead Railway
Artist: G. Hawkins
On Stone by: G. Hawkins
Lithographers: Day & Son
Date: 1850
From: E. Clark, *The Britannia and
  Conway Tubular Bridges*
Tinted Lithograph
Publisher: Russell, London

The first train passed over the
bridge in March 1850. The
bridge had claimed many lives.
The railway track was just over a
hundred feet above water and
the total length of the bridge was
over eighteen hundred feet. It
contained over one and a third
million cubic feet of masonry.
The artist and lithographer of
these four views, George Hawkins, has been compared with
Bourne by Sir Arthur Elton. His
views were published in the atlas
of folio-size plates that accompanied Edwin Clark's book on the
Britannia and Conway Bridges,
but they were also published
separately by Hawkins and by
the lithographer-publisher most
intimately associated with the
early railway age – Rudolf Ackermann.

Chepstow
South Wales Railway
Artist: Unknown
Date: About 1851
Black and White Lithograph
Publisher: Probably R. Taylor, Chepstow

The South Wales Railway's line from Swansea to Chepstow was opened on 18 June 1850. At about the same time as Chepstow Bridge was completed in 1851, joining the line to the rest of the railway network, the running of the South Wales Railway was leased to the Great Western. The line had already been exempted from the prohibition of further broad-gauge construction of 1845 and remained on the seven-foot gauge until 1872. Chepstow Station was built on a high embankment to the west of Brunel's spectacular bridge over the Wye. In this view, the work of an artist experienced in landscape but not railways can be seen.

Bridgend
South Wales Railway
Artist: Unknown
Date: About 1851
Coloured Lithograph
Publisher: Unknown

Bridgend had been joined to the Dyffryn Llynvi and Porthcawl Railway as early as 1834, but this was one of the many mineral lines of the early nineteenth century and not a common carrier. The line celebrated in this view is the South Wales Railway, authorized in 1845 and at one hundred and ninety-four miles the longest line approved in a single Act to that time. The train, and the locomotive in particular, seem to have presented the artist with problems of scale: the rolling stock is Great Western and broad gauge but bears little resemblance to Bourne's treatment of such subjects (see Plate 78).

The Interior of the General Railway Station, Chester
Artist: Unknown
Lithographers: J. Gresty, Chester
Date: 1864
From: J. Gresty, *Illustrated Chester*
Tinted Lithograph

From 1840, when the Chester and Birkenhead Railway was completed, Chester became an important railway junction, connected by 1854 to Holyhead, Shrewsbury, Crewe, Manchester and Merseyside. By 1864 the railway was so taken for granted that neither volumes of views nor individual prints could find a market. The only new lithographs of railway scenes appeared in illustrated works on particular localities, and this view is an example. It gives an impression of the concourse of a busy station. Part of an early carriage is visible on the left.

Malvern from the Link Railway
  Station
Worcester and Hereford Railway
Artist: Unknown
Lithographers: J. Newman & Co.
Date: About 1859
Tinted Lithograph
Publisher: H. Cross, Malvern

The Worcester and Hereford Railway was incorporated in 1853 and built a narrow-gauge line between the two towns via Malvern, a distance of just under thirty miles. The first section, which included Malvern Link Station, was opened in July 1859, and the line was completed in 1860 in which year it became part of the West Midland Railway. Malvern was also reached by the Tewkesbury and Malvern Railway in 1862. Although a resort already, the town became a centre for the education of the children of the wealthy and accessibility was made easier by the railway.

INDEX

The Viaduct over the River Spey
Inverness and Aberdeen
    Junction Railway
Artist: Unknown
Lithographers: Maclure,
    MacDonald & MacGregor
Date: About 1860
Tinted Lithograph

Long after the railway had become commonplace in the more populous regions, it was still penetrating the remote corners of the British Isles, and its arrival continued to be commemorated in prints. In the Highlands of Scotland, the railway reached Inverness in 1855. The Inverness and Aberdeen Junction Railway was a product of the amalgamation of two Inverness-based companies in 1858. In this view, one of the many large viaducts on the line is illustrated. On a small scale it seems to echo the Menai Tubular Bridge.